TRIPPING THE T
OF GHOS

"In his latest work, P. D. Newman builds upon his literary legacy into the domain of the ancient use of magical plant medicines in southeastern North America. A disciplined and visionary scholar, Newman ties the oral traditions and cosmologies of Indigenous peoples to carefully researched evidence of the use of mystical substances at sacred geographic sites. Newman has uncovered a secret connection between entheogenic and medicinal plants and the inspiration behind Mississippian iconography and cosmology. Indigenous spiritualists consumed these sacred medicines and looked to the cosmos to tell the story of the first humans, the Tree of Life, and the epic tales of the Thunder Twins—among many other mythological motifs. P. D. Newman raises the bar for Indigenous anthropologists and archaeologists to higher levels of thought regarding the formation and function of cosmology in ancient Native America."

TAYLOR KEEN (OMAHA/CHEROKEE),
AUTHOR OF *REDISCOVERING TURTLE ISLAND*

"P. D. Newman has written a remarkable and authoritative book that dramatically alters what we have long believed about Native American shamanism. He has masterfully uncovered and documented key aspects of the rituals involved in what is called the 'Path of Souls'—the journey of the souls of the departed to the sky world and beyond. For those interested in the practices and beliefs of Native American mound builders, this is a must-read book that answers long-concealed mysteries."

GREGORY L. LITTLE, AUTHOR OF *THE ILLUSTRATED ENCYCLOPEDIA OF NATIVE AMERICAN INDIAN MOUNDS & EARTHWORKS* AND COAUTHOR OF *ORIGINS OF THE GODS*

"P. D. Newman has produced a book with a rare and elusive combination of qualities: engaging, intellectually stimulating, and benefiting from sound scholarship and personal experience. His reconstruction of the interface between psychedelics and shamanic afterlife journeys among the Indigenous peoples of the Mississippi Valley is both inventive and original."

GREGORY SHUSHAN, PH.D., AUTHOR OF
NEAR-DEATH EXPERIENCE IN ANCIENT CIVILIZATIONS

TRIPPING THE TRAIL
OF GHOSTS

Psychedelics and the
Afterlife Journey
in Native American
Mound Cultures

P. D. NEWMAN

Inner Traditions

Rochester, Vermont

Inner Traditions
One Park Street
Rochester, Vermont 05767
www.InnerTraditions.com

Cataloging-in-Publication Data for this title is available from the Library of Congress

ISBN 979-8-88850-041-5 (print)
ISBN 979-8-88850-042-2 (ebook)

Printed and bound in the United States by Lake Book Manufacturing, LLC

10 9 8 7 6 5 4 3 2 1

Text design by Virginia Scott Bowman and layout by Priscilla Harris Baker
This book was typeset in Garamond Premier Pro with Futura, Gill Sans, and Gin
used as display typefaces

Figure 6.6 is in the public domain. Figure 8.3 is shared via CC BY-SA 3.0.

To send correspondence to the author of this book, mail a first-class letter to the
author c/o Inner Traditions • Bear & Company, One Park Street, Rochester, VT
05767, and we will forward the communication, or contact the author directly at
pdnewman83@gmail.com

Scan the QR code and save 25% at InnerTraditions.com.
Browse over 2,000 titles on spirituality, the occult, ancient
mysteries, new science, holistic health, and natural medicine.

◉◉◉

Dedicated to the loving memory of
Joshua David Coopwood—
see you in the Sky World, Brother.

CONTENTS

FOREWORD

By Christine VanPool

On December 13, 2022, I had a Facebook message from P. D. Newman, someone I did not know, stating, "Good morning. I am just discovering your research via the amazing George Lankford. Thank you for your important contributions." A smile broke across my face as I remembered hanging out with the amazing George Lankford years before at the Santa Fe Institute as we were called to discuss Amerindian cosmology and societies. Professor Emeritus Lankford is a well-known folklorist and a wonderful person. Anyone familiar with George was immediately high on my list! I responded to this new Facebook connection and began a fascinating discussion with P. D. as he shared his creative and insightful thoughts about Southeastern archaeology. Of special interest to me was P. D.'s suggestion that Mississippian people developed a hallucinogenic recipe that was chemically similar to the famous ayahuasca brew of South America. There are different plant recipes for ayahuasca, but at least two powerful alkaloids must be present: harmine (derived from *Banisteriopsis* spp.) and *N,N*-dimethyltryptamine (DMT or *N,N*-DMT) (from *Anadenanthera* spp. or *Psychotria viridis*)(VanPool 2019). Given my own archaeological work on entheogens and shamanism, I was intrigued by this suggestion! With as much energy and excitement as I could muster, I encouraged P. D. to pursue this idea. He explained to me how, in his *Missihuasca* hypothesis, Mississippian shamans could utilize hallucinogenic tobacco (*Nicotiana rustica*, with its harmine alkaloids, for example) alongside honey locust (*Gleditsia triacanthos*, with its *N,N*-DMT alkaloids) as well as other significant plants detailed in this book to produce a powerful plant medicine similar to those used by other cultures throughout the Americas and indeed around the world.

Academic archaeologists are a cantankerous lot. Sometimes I think we argue just to argue. (I'm pretty sure this is from working in the sun all day and then drinking a beer after work. Having a good, vigorous discussion is one of our favorite ways to keep ourselves entertained!) A topic that has been debated for at least three generations of archaeologists is the use and meaning of the term *shaman*. Some think it is a great term, others think it is useless outside of egalitarian hunting and gathering societies, and still others think it is completely impractical for archaeologists studying the past through rock, pots, and the other remnants of human behavior. I am not going to be able to settle this debate here, but my own view is that the archaeological record provides great insights into past religions. We often can identify religious and cosmological systems in which certain individuals act as intermediaries between their people and the spirits. These people are shamans, in my mind and in comparison to the ethnographic record.

Cross-culturally, shamans conduct rituals for a variety of reasons. While many scholars have focused on the medicinal/healing aspect of shamanism, shamans do more than heal individuals and communities. They perform rituals to predict and manipulate weather, predict the future, find lost animals and objects for clients, and find lost souls and return them to their owners (and yes, if you are wondering, soul loss is a form of sickness). They also explain songs and cultural stories to their people, for they are the knowledge and wisdom keepers of their tribes. Further, the archaeological and ethnographic records indicate that shamans conducted rituals to go into altered states of consciousness (ASC). To induce ASC, shamanic rituals often included fasting, chanting, clapping, dancing, drumming, and/or rattling. Entheogens are not necessary, but they are commonly used because particular plants produce specific experiences that are desired to achieve specific goals.

The differences in plant medicines give each entheogen its own "personality." Shamans worldwide tie these differences to each plant having its own spirits that can help the shamans and their clients. Some plants are cherished for their healing properties, while others are respected for their visionary capabilities. Elsewhere I have discussed sacred tobacco (*Nicotiana rustica*) and how it cleanses and protects people and ritual areas (VanPool and VanPool 2007). It is a powerful smudging agent, but it does so much more. When ritually consumed it allows one's soul to take flight as bird/human anthropomorph, making it an effective conduit to travel to the spirit world. Dangerous *Datura* spp., on the other hand, can be tricky, but they open the shaman's mind, allowing one to talk to deceased people. As a result, it is commonly used for ancestor worship (VanPool 2009).

I am not alone in thinking about how particular plants are used for specific purposes. Richard Evans Schultes and colleagues (1998) provide detailed discussions of many plant medicines and their uses and impacts. These and other discussions are tremendously useful, perhaps even essential, to understanding many past and present religious systems, but I have come to wonder if they may be incomplete. Except for ayahuasca and a few other brews, we typically do not consider "cocktail recipes" for plant medicines. Ethnographic examples and common sense, however, indicate that plant medicines can be and are mixed in various ways to produce desired effects. This is one of the key insights that P. D. brought to my attention, and one of the most important contributions he presents here in this book.

P. D. Newman carefully considers historic documents and archaeological evidence and compares these to his intimate and experiential knowledge of plants. In doing so, he adds another layer to Mississippian archaeology from a vantage point beyond just the archaeological record. He contends that ancient Mississippian shamans used what he calls *Missihuasca* (a combination of the words *Mississippian* and *ayahuasca*) plants to enable them to safely travel to the spirit world to better understand afterlife journeys. The ethnographic record indicates that death journeys weighed heavily on the minds of Native Americans in the Eastern Woodlands and on the Plains (Carr 2022), but we have not really considered how this might be reflected in ancient rituals. P. D.'s work here provides a nuanced understanding of how the plant medicines in the region might have been linked to these beliefs and in doing so expands on the insights provided in George Lankford's (2006) "The Path of Souls" and other soul travels (Carr 2022). *Missihuasca* as a conduit for cosmological traveling allowed Mississippian shamans to report to their people what to expect and how to navigate their bodily deaths as they faced the afterlife.

One of the dangers with "interpretive" studies is that we can lose sight of the empirical record and what we can actually "know." Going too far down an interpretive road without holding to some means of evaluating our ideas against the archaeological record can lead to odd conclusions, perhaps even culminating in theories about lost continents like Atlantis or extraterrestrial visitors. Having grown up near Roswell, New Mexico, I love a good alien story as much as the next person, but I prefer they stay out of my archaeological explanations! P. D. is an empiricist and does not fall into this trap. His attention to detail is clear from the following book, and all of his ideas can be evaluated by scientists. I sincerely look forward to seeing P. D.'s ideas being carefully considered, and I hope to do some of this work myself.

Not everyone agrees with my analytical definition of shamanism or my assessment of shamanic rituals. I stress in all my classes at the University of Missouri that, when possible, it is best to use the specific cultural terms for religious practitioners and place them in their own cultural contexts. Some ayahuasca shamans, for example, call themselves *vegetalistas*—little plant learners. If I am writing about Peruvian shamans, I will use their preferred term and link them to their cosmological frameworks that give their experiences meaning. Yet, we do not know what terms might have been used in the past, and it is through archaeological study that we understand the past. Thus, I find little objection to and much to be gained from the sorts of analyses

P. D. presents here. We cannot learn about the past without thinking about the past, and we cannot think about the past without having conceptual models to evaluate. I am certain that debating and evaluating P. D.'s model will clarify and sharpen our thinking. I hope you find P. D. Newman's ideas as tantalizing as I do.

CHRISTINE VANPOOL

COLUMBIA, MISSOURI

CHRISTINE S. VANPOOL earned her B.S. in anthropology at Eastern New Mexico University and her M.A. and Ph.D. in anthropology from the University of New Mexico. She is an associate professor of anthropology at the University of Missouri–Columbia. Her research focuses on the anthropology of religion, especially shamanism among Native Americans. Many of her analyses use shamanic art to examine the cognitive structure of religious practices across the New World, especially the North American Southwest and Mesoamerica. She has published over 60 peer-reviewed articles and books. Her works include "Ancient Medicinal Plants of South America" (2019, *Proceedings of the National Academy of Sciences*), *Signs of the Casas Grandes Shamans* (2007, University of Utah Press), and *An Anthropological Study of Spirits* (2023, Springer). She is also the coauthor of *Signs of the Casas Grandes Shamans*.

REFERENCES CITED

Carr, Christopher. *Being Scioto Hopewell: Ritual Drama and Personhood in Cross-cultural Perspective.* Cham, Switzerland: Springer Nature, 2022.

Lankford, George E. "The Path of Souls: Some Death Imagery in the Southeastern Ceremonial Complex." In *Ancient Objects and Sacred Realms: Interpretations of Mississippian Iconography*, edited by F. Kent Keilly and James F. Garber, 174–212. Austin, TX: University of Texas Press, 2006.

Schultes, Richard Evans, Albert Hofmann, and Christian Rätsch. *Plants of the Gods: Their Sacred, Healing, and Hallucinogenic Powers.* Rochester, VT: Healing Arts Press, 1998.

VanPool, Christine S. "The Signs of the Sacred: Identifying Shamans Using Archaeological Evidence." *Journal of Anthropological Archaeology* 28, no. 2 (2007): 177–190.

VanPool, Christine S. "Ancient Medicinal Plants of South America." *PNAS* 116, no. 23 (2019): 11087–11089.

VanPool, Christine S., and Todd L. VanPool. *Signs of the Casas Grandes Shamans*. Salt Lake City: University of Utah Press, 2007.

FINDING THE PATH OF SOULS

In the fall of 2022, having just finished writing my book *Theurgy: Theory and Practice: The Mysteries of the Ascent to the Divine*, I was invited to speak on the research presented in my previous work, *Angels in Vermilion: The Philosophers' Stone from Dee to DMT*, at a conference organized by the Tyringham Initiative and held at beautiful Broughton Hall Estate, located in the town of Skipton in North Yorkshire, England. Between presentations, while privately discussing my theurgy manuscript with one of the lecturers, Brian Muraresku, I was overheard by Dennis McKenna and Graham Hancock, conversing nearby, who asked if I was talking about something that I'd never heard of before: the Path of Souls. The Path of Souls is a Native American model of the afterlife journey that was shared by a number of Indigenous tribes throughout the Southeast during the Mississippian Period. Before the weekend was over, I had placed an order for a book on the subject, appropriately titled *Path of Souls: The Native American Death Journey*, by a fellow Memphian named Gregory Little. Inexplicably, the similarities between two metaphysical maps—from the perceived presence of a pair of portals secreted away in certain clusters of stars to the prevalent belief that the arch of the Milky Way was a heavenly highway leading to the Land of the Dead—were both stunning and undeniable. Over the next six months, in addition to Little's informative treatise, I digested virtually everything I could find on the subject of the Mississippian Ideological Interaction Sphere (MIIS)—especially anything published by members of the San Marcos School of Interpretation, which was born out of the Mississippian Iconographic Conference (MIC). Held annually or biannually at Texas State University since 1992, the MIC is hosted by the brilliant and passionate American anthropologist F. Kent Reilly III, and seeks to understand the function and meaning of the mysterious art and iconography of the MIIS. As I worked through seminal books like *Hero, Hawk, and Open Hand: American Indian Art of the Ancient Midwest and South*; *Ancient Objects and Sacred Realms: Interpretations of Mississippian Iconography*; and *Visualizing the Sacred: Cosmic Visions, Regionalism, and the Art of the Mississippian World*, it became increasingly evident that the Path of Souls paradigm wasn't envisaged as simply a journey to be taken by the soul after death. In reality, it was also a ritualized model of "shamanic" initiation intended to instill members of certain medicine sodalities with a firsthand knowledge of both supernatural entities and the Land of the Dead. That is, it was a virtual preparation for what was believed to be an inevitable reality for anyone who would dare to launch his soul directly into the heart of this mystery. The present book constitutes a meager sketch of those same initiatory modes of preparation.

P. D. Newman
Tupelo, Mississippi

ACKNOWLEDGMENTS

Contrary to a comment made by one of my favorite English Perennialists, no man constitutes an island universe. And this man is no exception. There are a number of important people whom I'd like to acknowledge for the hand they've had in the publication of this special book. First and foremost, I'd like to thank my amazing wife, Rebecca, for always supporting the trajectory of my work. I admit, it's gotten pretty fringe on more than one occasion—but you were there for it every time. I'd also like to salute my youngest son and indispensable research assistant, Bacchus, for consistently being ready to go on whatever adventure Papa might have in mind. You're a great sidekick. I'm especially grateful to my parents, Steve and Susan. You two have always motivated me to follow my curiosity, no matter where it may lead me. For always being trusty soundboards, I want to honor my dear friends, Lazarus Hawkins, Jaime Lamb, Kelly Ervin, Justin Ross, Tom Hatsis, and Khalil Reda. My favorite brother has also been indispensable in this regard (I love you, Michael). Without y'all, I'd just be talking to myself. I'm thankful, too, for the friendly encouragement and advice I received from three of my own personal inspirations—Eric Singleton, David Dye, and Chris VanPool. I appreciate you all for your good counsel and sound advice. Even though we've never met, I'd also like to recognize Robert Hall, George Lankford, Jim Brown, and Kent Reilly. Were it not for the ingenuity shown by you four exceptional men, I would not have had a book to write. Gratitude must also be expressed for the memory of Keewaydinoquay Pakawakuk Peschel. It is only on account of her courage and fortitude that the world has not forgotten the sacred name of Miskwedo. Thank you also to Anjie Rivero for the stunning, evocative artwork. It really makes the book "pop." Penultimately, I am grateful to the one and only Greg Little. It was your remarkable treatise on the Path of Souls that really opened my eyes to the whole MIIS phenomenon in the first place. Finally, and most importantly, I wish to pay my ultimate respects to the Native communities of Southeastern North America. To quote Sioux adoptee Frithjof Schuon: "What one can give to the Indians is strengthening light and what one can receive from them is luminous strength."

◎◎◎

"Our brother! Soon you will be there in the Land of Souls. You will see your ancestors and your brothers and sisters. Already they are preparing a reception for your arrival. The men are hunting and fishing; the women are setting up your lodge and making clothes for you. When you arrive everything will be ready; and the spirits will celebrate the Festival of a New Arrival. And then you, too, will await the arrival of your wife and children.

"But before you arrive in the Land of Souls you must walk the Path of Souls. You must be careful. The trials that you endured on this Path of Life are over—but you will encounter new ones on every hill and at every bend along the Path of Souls. You are being tested. Be strong. Do not weaken.

"Listen, our brother! The tests that you will meet on the way are different from the ones that you suffered on earth. Here, they are direct and easily recognized. Although they were sometimes sudden, they were easily repelled. But the tests that you will face on the Path of Souls are not so plain. They are subtle, disguised in innocence. They are much more dangerous than any that you may have encountered in this life.

"Remember. Walk alone; eat by yourself; sleep with no one. Do this, even though there are hardships. You will be hungry and you will be cold. You will be lonely and you will be tired. You will be thirsty and you will be afraid. Your spirit will be weak. And when it is weak, the tests will appear.

"They will seem harmless. There may be a feast in a village to which you will be invited. Do not go: it is the Feast of Death. There may be a night camp in which people are preparing for

sleep. Do not stop: it is the Sleep of Death. If you come upon a campfire, do not warm yourself: it is the Fire of Death. If you see a brook, do not drink of it: it is the Water of Death. Should you come upon someone lying in the ground, leave him: it is the Agony of Death. Whatever you see or hear—pass it by.

"Our brother! Be on guard! Have a safe journey!"

BASIL JOHNSTON, *Ojibway Ceremonies*

MEET THE MIIS-SISSIPPIANS

The Mississippian Ideological Interaction Sphere (MIIS) refers to a mysterious complex of mythological, ceremonial, and iconographic motifs shared by people in a number of different regions in Southeastern North America from approximately 800 CE to 1600 CE. Successors to the Hopewell culture, the Mississippians were responsible for creating, maintaining, and embellishing many of the enigmatic platform mounds and earthworks constructed in and around the Mississippi Valley—the awe-inspiring remains of which are exhibited to this day throughout the Southeastern landscape of North America.[1] Beginning around 1200 BP, the Mississippian culture first emerged from the middle Mississippi River Valley, exhibiting vibrant and creative lifeways that persisted right up to the seventeenth century CE. The Natives of this period and place are perhaps best known for their textile, artistic, and agrarian innovations, such as, for instance, their remarkably durable shell-tempered pottery, their cold-hammered, paper-thin copper repoussé plates, their expertly carved whelk shell gorgets and cups, and a groundbreaking horticultural technique that grew out of their almost universal incorporation of maize—known as the three sisters method of planting. Other acceptable names for this fascinating and resourceful demographic include the Mississippian Art and Ceremonial Complex (MACC), the somewhat outdated Southeastern Ceremonial Complex (SECC),[2] and the admittedly inappropriate Southern Death Cult. None of these titles, however, live up to the beauty, grandeur, and sheer mystique of which many of the Mississippian sites and artifacts are possessed.

The first time I laid eyes upon one of these impressive structures, I was in northern Mississippi, driving up the Natchez Trace Parkway (the famous route along which a young, pregnant Shoshone interpreter would guide two Freemasons from the Corps of Discovery following the Louisiana Purchase) toward Nashville, Tennessee, when a curious sight caught my eye: four acute yet miniature Tor-like hills, all bulging out from the luscious landscape like some uniform series of grassy Benben stones. I say miniature, but that's only in comparison with the Torr—in truth, many of these monuments are positively gargantuan. Parking my '94 Ford Tempo next to the display kiosk maintained by the National Park Service, I exited the vehicle and made the first of what would become a great many fascinated and entranced treks out onto the hot, humid, holy grounds of what I now know to call the "Pharr Mounds."

The Pharr Mounds constitute one of eleven or twelve major mound sites still located in the Hospitality State. While it was the preceding Hopewell culture who erected those earthworks during the Middle Woodland period, in addition to creating a number of their own impressive structures, the Mississippian peoples both maintained and often altered many of the mounds left behind by their prolific predecessors. Some Mississippian mounds faithfully adhere to their Woodland, Formative, and Archaic prototypes. More often, though, the Hopewells' successors favored platform pyramid-style—and later, circular platform—mounds. Many of the latter were erected directly atop preexisting mounds, grafted on in a "sidecar" fashion. Two excellent examples of megalithic Mississippian mound sites still found in the Hospitality State include the enormous Emerald (not to be confused with the Emerald Acropolis, to which we'll return below) and Winterville Mounds—both located in the southern half of Mississippi. Other notable sites utilized by the same post-Hopewellian culture but found outside of the Twentieth State include the gargantuan Cahokia

Mounds State Historic Site found in Collinsville, Illinois, the spectacular Spiro Mounds Archaeological Center of Oklahoma, the equally extravagant Etowah Indian Mounds State Historic Site erected in Cartersville, Georgia, and the monumental Moundville Archaeological Park in Alabama.

In addition to the more familiar heap-style mounds, such as the phenomenal Pharr Mounds described above, many ceremonial sites of the Mississippi Valley—including the impressive "Mound I" of the Owl Creek Mounds near Houston, Mississippi—are stylized rather as terrene trapezoids, giving off the distinct visual impression of truncated earthen pyramids. Most Southerners are accustomed to seeing them, although against the rustic, meridional countryside these megalithic structures seem to the traveling tourist wholly out of place, as though they'd be more at home a bit farther toward the austral, in Mexico or South America—or perhaps even in Egypt, which can scarcely be conjured independently of the inevitable invocation of the Great Pyramid at Giza. Nevertheless, as an ironic aside, it is worth noting that the base of the famous Monk's Mound at Cahokia is roughly the same size as that of the Great Pyramid—and larger even than the Mexican Pyramid of the Sun at Teotihuacan. Moreover, in the vicinities of several of these sacred sites, on top of the oft-found incinerated and intact skeletal remains of what are believed to have been village elites and even the occasional human sacrifice, were found ancient artifacts bearing a number of caringly carved and painted abstract, anthropomorphic, and zoomorphic symbols. These include fire-breathing skulls, hands with "eyes" in their palms, winged serpents and serpents having antlers, aquatic panthers (also having antlers), and giant raptors—all pertaining to what the San Marcos School of archaeological interpretation believes to be an early Native American model for the after-death journey, known colloquially as the "Path of Souls."[3] But it is my contention that the manipulation of this potent and productive iconography transcends the domain of the merely mortuary and merges with the mystical and magical modes of endemic medicine known as shamanism. In the following chapters, I will argue that this postmortem rite of passage in fact doubles as an elaborate initiatory system, dramatically ritualized and centered around a number of powerful visionary concoctions.

Central to the MIIS was this puzzling set of iconographic symbols, many of which were shared with the preceding Hopewell, Adena, and Poverty Point cultures—the hand and the raptor, for instance, were known to the Hopewell. Conversely, a number of these images appear to be completely unknown to those archaic cultures that arrived before the MIIS. Executed in a number of regional stylistic variations, the set of symbols comprising the Path of Souls cycle functioned in a manner analogous to that of books of the dead in other cultures.[4] According to American anthropologist F. Kent Reilly III,

> Hemphill engraved pottery excavated at Moundville shows signs of use, which strongly suggests that these vessels were not solely intended as grave goods. Perhaps containing sacred medicine, they were used in a variety of rituals that emphasized the ideology of the Path of Souls. Indeed, at Moundville Hemphill pottery with its engraved motifs may have functioned as an analog to the Book of the Dead in other cultures. In this hypothesis, each Hemphill vessel contained powerful medicine that would assist the soul of the deceased on the path to overcome the tribulations that the supernatural entity engraved on the bottle represents.[5]

Mississippian iconography differed, however, from standard mortuary texts in that some Path of Souls artifacts—namely, the pipes, pots, and drinking vessels—were both practical and virtually interactive. Indeed, by virtue of their consecrated contents, these pieces were possessed of the power to invoke the supernatural depicted on the pot or pipe, projecting their smoker(s) and drinker(s) directly into these particular powers' precincts—those domains being various important points plotted along the Path of Souls.[6] Reilly continues,

> [The] placement of the Great Serpent imagery on specific vessel forms (often bottles in the [Lower Mississippi Valley]) assuredly

functioned to manifest a supernatural power that otherwise could not be seen. Imagery could, for example, have identified a vessel as containing special substances, sacred contents, or perhaps ritual "medicine" used in ceremonies in which the Great Serpent acted as the major supernatural. These symbols would have triggered memory on a cosmic scale, much as on a more pedestrian level the "Rx" symbol and instructions on the label of a prescribed medication alert a patient today to the contents of a small orange plastic bottle. The image of the Great Serpent on a pottery vessel very well may have identified the medicine it contained, while linking it with specific rituals that this supernatural controlled.[7]

The specific rituals to which each of the shell cups are linked were both initiatory and graded, meaning that the cup in one's possession, with its particular iconography, also served as a badge of attainment—an indication to other members of the society of one's rank and degree within the medicine sodality. A Creek legend concerning a young boy's initiatory descent to the cave of the Tie-snakes, located in the Below World—no doubt reflective of an actual Indigenous male rite of passage—confirms this correlation. An entry titled, "Journey to the Underwater Lodge," an important tale in American folklorist George E. Lankford's book *Native American Legends of the Southeast*, begins: "A chief sent his son with a message to another chief, and delivered to him a vessel as the emblem of his authority."[8] The drinking cup served as the chief's badge of attainment. The folklorist appropriately comments on this Creek charter, saying that,

> Archaeologists may find intriguing this reference to a custom of sending a bowl as an ambassadorial gift, for it suggests a reason other than trade for the presence of "exotic" ceramics at sites in the Southeast.[9]

Indeed, it suggests that, far more than simple objects of trade, marine shell cups, gorgets, and pieces of pottery that were carved, formed, and incised to reflect certain supernatural, nonhuman entities could also serve an important etiological function within the society. In this case, they communicated the level of one's personal advancement along the virtual postmortem Path that every initiate must ultimately walk. This also explains why those in possession of such valuable vessels were regularly interred with them. They were quite literally a part of their possessor's identity.

From culture to culture, both ancient and modern, the afterlife journey is oftentimes envisaged as a heroic postmortem rite of passage, replete with ordeals, trials, and tribulations that the struggling soul must overcome; challenges through which the dead must pass if he is to reach the Land of the Dead. In almost every case, this etheric excursion ultimately culminates in the eventual incorporation of the soul of the deceased into the realm of the ancestors or the Land of the Dead. Of course, depending on regional variations, reincarnation or total oblivion may also sometimes be alternative possibilities. Terminal trips of this sort have become familiar to us in the skeptical West through exotic, popularized magical spell and ritual mortuary texts, such as the misnomered Egyptian Book of the Dead and the equally misnomered Tibetan Book of the Dead, and via even more obscure lineages of mystical transmission, such as the controversial yet no less traditional teaching of the Aerial Toll Houses in the Eastern Orthodox Christian Church. The Native American afterlife journey known as the Path of Souls constituted one such metaphysical mortuary map, although, as I have said, it also served as an effective model of initiation and spiritual attainment.

The conceptualization of the Land of the Dead in the MIIS was a lot like the notion of Hades ascribed to the Ancient Greeks. The only souls allowed entry into Hades were those whose mortal bodies were no longer animate—that is, they were physically dead. If they weren't actually deceased, therefore, they wouldn't be getting in. Moreover, once they were in, there was no chance of getting out. Multiple Greek myths reflect this paradigm. To ensure that those rules and restrictions were enforced, Hades was stationed with a ferocious guardian named Cerberus—a three-headed "hellhound"—who policed the halls of

Hades to ensure that its infernal boundaries were not breached. Instead of a tricephalic canine, the Land of the Dead in the Mississippian model was reinforced by a supernatural entity known as the Great Serpent—an enormous snake equipped with the feathered wings of an eagle and an enormous, intimidating red-colored eye. This serpentine monster closely guarded the gate leading onto the Path of Souls.

There are purportedly two major entries leading the dead onto the Path of Souls. Each of these portals corresponds to a point in the night sky at which the ecliptic (the path through which the sun and planets appear to move through the zodiac wheel on their cyclical diurnal and annual courses) intersects with the bow-like band of stars arching over the heavens—recognized by Westerners as the Milky Way galaxy. One of those portals is accessible at the north end of the arc in and around the summer solstice, and the other, in the south, at the time surrounding the winter solstice. Originally, at Cahokia, only the northern summer portal appears to have been utilized—and that solely by the souls of actual expired elites who, in life, possessed the secretive knowledge of the Path and its portal. Not unlike in ancient Egypt, where, in the beginning, only the pharaohs were permitted to proceed to the afterlife, not everyone had the opportunity to enter the Land of the Dead. Later, however, with the development of soul-projecting techniques induced by deep trance, those who did possess the initiated secrets of the Path of Souls began guiding the spirits of the uninitiated—that is, they evolved into a secretive sodality of shamanic psychopomps who, for a nominal fee, would guide a person or a person's loved one(s) along the Path of Souls and into the exclusive Land of the Dead. Something similar took place in ancient Egypt, when the *Pyramid Texts*, originally proprietary to the ruling pharaohs, began being painted and sold on the inside of common coffins—at which point this initiated wisdom became known as the *Coffin Texts*. Finally, in the end, basically anybody who wanted one could have their own personal Book of the Dead.

Significantly, while it was found at virtually every other Mississippian site, there wasn't a single example of Great Serpent iconography recovered from Cahokia. Why is that? They were certainly aware of the concept, for, as we shall learn, images of it are found formed on the walls of Picture Cave—the veritable birthplace of the MIIS. Indeed, even the earlier Hopewell Indians left monuments to this intimidating being, including, for instance, the impressive Serpent Mound found in Peebles, Ohio—the same of which happens to align perfectly with the sunset on the summer solstice. There was no Great Serpent iconography recovered from Cahokia because, at that early time in the Mississippian Era, this "Dweller on the Threshold," to borrow a term from Sir Edward Bulwer-Lytton, wasn't really a threat, for the only persons attempting to access the Path during that formative period were the initiated elite. According to American archaeologist William F. Romain, the Cahokians accessed the Path of Souls via the northern gate in and around the summer solstice, when the Milky Way galaxy aligned perfectly with a certain burial mound found at the site. However, by the time the necropolis of Moundville emerged, Lankford informs us that it was primarily the southern gate that was being exploited, and that during the winter solstice. This interesting fact is a good indication that the Great Serpent of the northern gate was intentionally being avoided.

The winter months for the Mississippians were largely a time of myth sharing and learning—a period for gathering the impressionable young around a communal fire, while beloved and wise hoary elders told timeless tales about the supernatural entities who held sway over the MIIS world. For it was considered a grave taboo to discuss the spirits outside of wintertime, lest one be overheard by these supernatural entities. This was especially true in regard to the Great Serpent, who, as the constellation recognized by Westerners as Scorpius, polices the summer night skies for any sign of uninitiated souls attempting to traverse the Path—his large, red eye (Antares) watching the skies intently for transgressors. Once summertime had gone, however, the Great Serpent became far less of a threat. Indeed, in the cold of winter, the sign of the scorpion is never seen ascending above the line of the horizon and into the night sky. During that time, assuming the appearance of an "Underwater Panther," the Winged Serpent is said to shed his locative feathers and, like a bear retiring to a cave for winter, descends into the

Below World for the duration of the season. It was for this very reason that Native American funerary rites for the uninitiated were not to be performed until after the heat of the summer—and thus the Winged Serpent—had passed. In the event that an uninitiated tribesman did meet his mortal end outside of the special time appointed, his bones were neatly bundled and stored until the following winter, when the necessary funerary rites could be correctly performed. During that dormancy period, the soul may be forced to "camp" at the edge of the earth disk, awaiting the approach of the proper solstitial season. Then, with a shamanic psychopomp as his guide, the soul of the recently deceased Native American embarked upon this dangerous, terrifying journey, cautiously setting foot upon the Milky Way's Path of Souls.[10]

For those entering the northern portal during the summer months, on the other hand, the point of entry was essentially believed to be the body of the Great Serpent himself, found in the zodiacal sign of the scorpion. Something similar was envisaged by the ancient Maya, who are said to have accessed the "White Road" of the Milky Way, leading the soul to the Land of the Dead, by entering the mouth of the "White-Bone-Snake."[11] The southern portal, however, open only in midwinter, is located at the direct opposite end of the sky. From November 29 to April 25, the stellar configuration recognized by modern Westerners as the constellation Orion is visible and identifiable in the night sky. Of course, while the Mississippians did not acknowledge it as the sign of the Hunter—a Greek convention—the eye-catching constellation was sacred to them, nonetheless, only, where we tend to see the three linear stars in the configuration as the Hunter's "belt," the Natives of Southeastern North America tended instead to view that same astral segment as the wrist-line of a different constellation altogether—known in the MIIS as the Hand Star or the Chief's Hand. Equally important for the Maya, this set of stars was imagined in the form of a turtle having three linear stars along the back of his shell. In the Mississippian mind, however, it was to this manus-like constellation that the aforementioned "disembodied hands with 'eyes' in their palms" alluded, although it is notable that this is an "eye" in form only, with its distinct vulvar, *vesica piscis*–like shape indicating rather an object known to select Natives as a sacred *mégis* or cowrie shell.[12] According to the Ojibwa, for example, it was through just such a sacred shell that the Creator initially breathed life and soul into the First Man.[13] Carried in the open palms by initiates of the Midéwiwin or "Grand Medicine Society," a secret society composed of shamans, the mégis is further symbolic of something called an ogee—an eye socket–like portal located in the "palm" of the Hand Star constellation (i.e., Orion) through which the soul of the dead (and of the spirit-journeying shaman) must be launched, arrow-like, if it is to embark upon the treacherous and challenging Path of Souls. Once he had penetrated the mégis-ogee in the palm, the ghostly traveler had officially set foot upon the Path that ultimately led to the Land of the Dead. The first leg of the journey therefore takes the soul westward, in the direction of the setting sun, where he is forced to attempt that fearsome leap of faith.

◎ ◎ ◎

Fig. I.1. Ogee bowl.

Photo by the author

The final leg of the journey along the Path of Souls is marked by an encounter with an impartial and formidable avian judge who manifested in the form of the great and threatening Raptor on the Path. As the constellation of Cygnus, the Raptor on the Path occupies a position on the Milky Way known to modern Westerners as the dark rift—a precarious "fork in the road," one way of which leads ultimately to the Land of the Dead, while the other is effectively a dead end that literally drops off into the blackness of space. In fact, indicative of this fork, the Raptor on the Path is often depicted with what archaeologists have termed the forked eye motif, the "eye" of Cygnus being the visible star, Deneb, the brightest in the birdlike constellation—located precisely at the point that constitutes this fork appearing in the Path of Souls. While the narrowing Path continues onward to the right, the lefthand pathway quite literally culminates in a drop-off. There, at the fork in the galaxy, if the soul was judged unfavorably by the Raptor on

◎ ◎ ◎
Fig. I.2. Panther effigy bowl.
Photo by the author

the Path, he was unknowingly directed toward the short path to the left, and from thence the unfortunate soul was forced to fall from this judiciary station at the "top of the sky," resigned to the watery Below World beneath—where the Underwater Panther lies in wait. On the other hand, in the event that a soul received a favorable judgment, the Raptor on the Path opened the route to the right-hand pathway, leading the soul safely to the Land of the Dead.

Of course, not all scholars accept Lankford's loose reconstruction of the Path of Souls model. Indeed, in an attempt to focus on the more universal characteristics of the journey, I myself have omitted a number of factors from Lankford's hypothetical conclusions. As American anthropological archaeologist Christopher Carr has correctly pointed out,

"[While] Lankford's writings distill some of the more common aspects of historic Woodland and Plains Indian narratives about afterlife journeys, [his] study misattributed commonality to other features of the journey."[14]

I would be inclined to agree with Carr in this case. These features include, for example, "the serpent bridge that can be difficult to cross" and, more especially, the two "ferocious dogs that attack the journeyer"—neither of which appear to be universal among those who subscribe to the Path of Souls model. I have omitted both the serpent bridge and the pair of ferocious dogs, therefore, from the present study.

However, are "directions for the dead" really all that this series of icons comprised? Yes and no. The answer is yes insofar as the Path of Souls symbol set actually does qualify as a chart for the "checked out." Like a list of foreboding landmarks, the icons representing the Path of Souls are supposed to be followed sequentially—a spiritual schematic of sorts. However, the answer is also no in that it probably wasn't a journey reserved exclusively for the deceased. Nor was it taken all at once in every case. In the form of an organized degree structure, appearing as certain sacred visualizations, ecstatic spirit journeys, and dramatic initiatory rites of passage, the Path of Souls was presumably traipsed by priest, prince, and polity alike—that is, it was doubtless trodden by both shaman and chief, as well as by members of an elite phratry or medicine sodality—*while they were still alive*.[15] Well, not really *alive*—but not exactly *dead* either; suspended somewhere between the two in a liminal, entranced state brought on by fasting, sleep deprivation, ritual activity, bodily mutilation, and prolonged participation in rhythmic drum and dance. This profoundly significant ceremony would have taken the form of a formally staged, ritualized mythodrama, specifically designed to pass an individual *nominally* and *virtually* through the very same trials expected to be encountered *really* on the Path of Souls. This was the initiation undergone by the elite. For that is precisely what the shamanic journey is understood to be—a magical death.[16] Leaving his cumbersome, corpse-like body behind by the potency of the rite, the soul of the shaman was rendered free to roam the realms of the spirits and enter the Land of the Dead. Moreover, upon his return to the land of the living, anticipated boons of wisdom and power were understood to follow closely in the healer-seer's wake.

One of the strongest arguments for the ritualization of Path of Souls iconography and myth comes from the Midéwiwin ritual known as Bear's Journey—the route taken by Makwa (Bear) Manitou in his delivery of the sacred bundles that resulted in the creation of the Midé Society and its rites. In the rituals of the Midéwiwin presented by American ethnologist Walter James Hoffman, it is Otter who is first initiated into its mysteries and brings the society to the Ojibwa.

> Mi'nabō'zho instructed the Otter in the mysteries of the Midē'wiwin, and gave him at the same time the sacred rattle to be used at the side of the sick; the sacred Midē' drum to be used during the ceremonial of initiation and at sacred feasts, and tobacco, to be employed in invocations and in making peace. [. . .] Then Mi'nabō'zho built a Midē'wigan (sacred Midē' lodge), and taking his drum he beat upon it and sang a Midē' song . . . [. . .] Mi'nabō'zho then took Otter into the Midē'wigan and conferred upon him the secrets of the Midē'wiwin, and with his Midē' bag shot the sacred mī'gis into his body that he might have immortality and be able to confer these secrets to his kinsmen, the Aníshinâ'bēg.[17]

⊚ ⊚ ⊚

Fig. I.3. Otter is an important supernatural in the Ojibwa cosmology.
See also color plate 1.

Illustration by A. Rivero; Vix Volante Creative

"Otter symbolized new life," says philosopher Michael Pomedli. "During the Mide performance," he continues, "the neophyte was shot with shells from an otter-skin medicine bag," which is "the most spectacular, and one of the most important, parts of the ceremony."[18]

According to American anthropologist Ruth Landes's Ojibwa informant, Pindigegizig (Hole-in-the-Sky), however, Bear is cited as the deliverer of the rites. And indeed, "Bear," writes Pomedli, "is the predominant figure on all levels of the Midewiwin."[19]

⊙ ⊙ ⊙

Fig. I.4. Makwa Manitou, the Bear supernatural of the Ojibwa.
See also color plate 2.

Illustration by A. Rivero; Vix Volante Creative

Bear's journey was so important to the Midé Society that it was dramatically ritualized during rites of initiation by various Midé-styled medicine societies, with members closely acting out the Manitou's route, step by step. Truly, in the form of a sacred Midéwiwin birch-bark scroll, a detailed diagram of Bear's journey was transmitted to Landes by her generous Ojibwa informant. This record describes the arrival of Makwa to the Middle World domain, where he delivered to the Ojibwa his sacred "Midé packs"—that is, the sacred bundles relative to Bear's medicine rites. Notably, his circuit from and back to his place of origin involves the passage of various significant landmarks ("points")—including the Manitou's eventual encounter with the supernatural mégis—to arrive at which he must cross a large body of water wherein the enormous, miraculous shell floats. Just like the souls of the psychopompic shamans and those of the recently deceased elites, it is imperative that Bear makes contact with the mégis—ensuring his passage to his divine destination. For the legend itself provides the necessary instruction relevant to those who would repeat the Manitou's ursic travels. It is not surprising, then, that Makwa's circuit was ritually repeated by initiates of various medicine lodges, with the same landmarks being deliberately included in the ceremonial layout of certain mound sites. A fine example is the topography of the Aetna Earthworks, in Missaukee County, Michigan, which closely mirrors the route taken by Makwa Manitou as he made his travels throughout the Middle World—with Western Enclosure 20MA11 and Eastern Enclosure 20MA12 standing in place of two of the landmarks prominently displayed upon Pindigegizig's Midé scroll.

Bear begins his travels in a large circle labeled Our Earth, "what we are sitting on." Within this sphere is a drawing of a mountain. Bear exits east and travels clockwise to the Big Earth, sketched as another large sphere. At Missaukee, there is a western earthwork (20MA11) that has a large boulder in its center. This boulder brings a physicality to this enclosure, and is possibly an emblem of Our Earth, "what we are sitting on"; the boulder is the counterpart of the mountain in the ethnographic drawing. This enclosure has an eastern exit, just as Bear exited east when he left Our Earth, "what we are sitting on." Bear then travels east to "Big Earth." At Missaukee there is another enclosure east of the western enclosure. While the two enclosures are similar in diameter, the eastern enclosure (20MA12) is larger, with a diameter of fifty-three meters versus a forty-eight-meter diameter for the western enclosure (20MA11). Moreover, the ditch and embankment of the eastern enclosure (20MA12) is more substantial in both height and width than the western enclosure (20MA11). This corresponds with "Big Earth" lying east of Our Earth, "what we are sitting on," in the ethnohistoric diagram. The travel continues with Bear leaving "Big Earth" to the west and looking into the Surrounding Ocean. He travels to lookout "points" to the north and south of the Surrounding Ocean. Seeing nothing he returns to the ocean and, with Lion's help, he continues westward into the Surrounding Ocean. Outside the entrance of the eastern enclosure (20MA12) is the upland spring and associated wetland area corresponding to the location of the Surrounding Ocean. Furthermore, at Missaukee the ground rises notably to the north and south of the eastern enclosure (20MA12) and the spring, paralleling the location of the lookout points north and south of "Big Earth" and the Surrounding Ocean in Bear's journey. Throughout Bear's travels from Our Earth, "what we are sitting on" to "Big Earth," and through the Surrounding Ocean, he stops at specific activity areas or stations, including the Ocean bottom. Bear repeatedly returns to some of these activity areas. Outside of the enclosures we found dispersed activity areas or "stations," and this pattern matches the pattern of discrete stops in the ethnographic account and diagram of Bear's journey. We also have archaeological evidence that at least one, and likely all, of these "stations" were used repeatedly.[20]

Bear's journey is an early version of the very model that contributed to the development of the Path of Souls cycle. The earthworks were, therefore, themselves a virtual training ground for the Path of Souls journey, aiding members of medicine societies in the internalization of the precise process the dead must know to execute if they are to finally arrive at the Land of the Dead.

However, as if powerful, dramatic ritual weren't extreme enough, evidence suggests that the potent trance induction techniques that accompanied such rituals were not employed alone but were in fact used by the Natives of the MIIS in conjunction with perhaps a number of different entheogenic teas and smoking blends. "While under the influence of a hallucinogen," reports Romain, "the individual may experience vivid sensations of flight, as well as transformations into other life forms." "Through their effects," he adds, "hallucinogenic substances allow one to experience flight to the upperworld and descent to the lowerworld, and engage in conversations with animals, spirit beings, and deceased persons."[21] While so-called "desert" tobacco and the infamous peyote cactus will no doubt be familiar to most as important Amerindian sacramental plants, Indigenous use of most of the entheogenic drugs discovered in and around a number of Mississippian sites, with the exception of tobacco, may be largely unknown to the casual reader. These Indigenous intoxicants include *Datura* spp., black nightshade, LSD-related morning glory spp.,[22] and even the makings for an as-yet-undocumented Mississippian analogue to the South American psychedelic potation *ayahuasca*—a concoction that I'm tentatively terming *Missihuasca*, involving the *N,N*-DMT-rich roots of the honey locust tree and the harmine-containing vines of the passion flower, among other possible plants containing monoamine oxidase inhibitors (MAOIs). There is ample evidence that "magic" mushrooms may also have been used. All of these powerful narcotic plants will be discussed in due course. But for those not familiar with the history of the use of tobacco and especially peyote among Native Americans, a brief description is in order.

ONE

NATIVE AMERICAN INTOXICANTS

While its utilization in the Americas stretches back deep into the opaque mists of prehistory, tobacco use was first documented in the late fifteenth century CE, with Christopher Columbus's fateful arrival on the beaches of the American continent. Observing its usage among the Taino Arawak tribe of modern-day Florida and the Caribbean, who would send their prayers aloft upon exhaled clouds of malty *Nicotiana rustica* smoke, the Italian explorer procured samples of tobacco, which returned with him to Spanish shores. It wouldn't be long before tobacco pipes, cigars, chews, and snuffs would begin showing up in virtually every major European market. However, where Indigenous Americans, by an ancient safeguard of ritual and myth, were largely insulated from the very real potential of its negative effects, European enthusiasts' uninhibited, chronic consumption and abuse of this new, exotic drug were enough to obscure any sense of the sacred, which tobacco at one time possessed. Long before the arrival of the Spanish and French, though, many Native American tribes told origin stories in regard to tobacco. But among the Amerindians of the Eastern Woodlands, there appears to have been but a single surviving, legendary tale. In his important book, *Native American Legends of the Southeast*, Lankford—who perhaps more than any other academic has labored for the preservation and understanding of Southeastern Native American cultures—relayed the Yuchi variation of this timeworn tale.

A man and a woman went into the woods. The man had intercourse with the woman and the semen fell upon the ground. From that time they separated, each going his own way. But after a while the woman passed near the place again, and thinking to revisit the spot, went there and beheld some strange weeds growing upon it. She watched them a long while. Soon she met the man who had been with her, and said to him, "Let us go to the place and I will show you something beautiful." They went there and saw it. She asked him what name to call the weeds, and he asked her what name she would give them. But neither of them would give a name. Now the woman had a fatherless boy, and she went and told the boy that she had something beautiful. She said, "Let us go and see it."

When they arrived at the place she said to him, "This is the thing that I was telling you about." And the boy at once began to examine it. After a little while he said, "I'm going to name this." Then he named it "tobacco." He pulled up some of the weeds and carried them home carefully and planted them in a selected place. He nursed the plants and they grew and became ripe. Now they had a good odor and the boy began to chew the leaves. He found them very good, and in order to preserve the plants he saved the seeds when they were ripe. He showed the rest of the people how to use the tobacco, and from the seeds which he preserved, all got plants and raised the tobacco for themselves.[1]

Tobacco is believed to be one of the first plants used by New World shamans to initiate ecstatic trance.[2] The charter cited above only mentions chewing the substance. There are a number of modes of consuming tobacco, however, that do not involve chewing, such as eating or drinking, insufflating, applying it topically in the form of salves or poultices, through an enema, and so on—although German anthropologist Johannes Wilbert found that of the 300 South American groups he studied who used tobacco, 233 of them felt that smoking was the most effective—and the most preferred—method of use.[3]

Indigenous tobacco, which is several times more potent than

commercial tobacco, could also be used by shamans for the purpose of communicating with spirits and with the Land of the Dead, even transporting the seer himself into the delirious domain of the deceased. Truly, ingesting excessive quantities of nicotine can actually cause the heart rate to lower to such a degree that a pulse becomes virtually inde- tectable. This results in critical catatonia and ultimately in a somatic rigidity that simulates the effects of rigor mortis. For all practical purposes, the tobacco-intoxicated shaman appears as though he were dead, during which spell his spirit is understood to have quite literally vacated his lifeless body.[4] Moreover, this induced death-state was not always simulated but was actually "an ever-present threat" when visit- ing that great realm.[5] In less extreme cases, unlike common commercial cigarettes, chew, or skoal, varieties of tobacco like *Nicotiana rustica* and *Nicotiana obtusifolia*, at correctly regulated dosages, completely wipe out the optical color system in humans, resulting in haunting, ghostlike visuals, where everything one looks upon appears only in black, white, and dingy yellow hues.[6] Beyond a simple recreational drug, tobacco was universally hailed among Native American tribes as a medicine, an apo- tropaic, an offering, a mode of shamanic flight, and even as an essential means of prayer. It is needed, for example, to begin an official "Half Moon" peyote ceremony.[7]

   As with tobacco, the historical usage among Native Americans of the *Lophophora williamsii* cactus (formerly *Anhalonium lewinii*), bet- ter known by its Nahuatl name, *peyōtl*—literally meaning "caterpillar cocoon"—is assuredly archaic, but that makes it no less unknown to us. White men's knowledge of the Amerindian application of this so-called whiskey root[8] doesn't begin until the end of the nineteenth century, when a Norwegian ethnographer named Carl Lumholtz went off in search of the descendants of the original Puebloan people.[9] What he finally found, tucked away in the most inaccessible canyons of the Sierra Madre, was a reclusive tribe of devout cactophiles calling themselves the Tarahumara. Making sheep or goat sacrifices to the visionary cactus, burning costly copal resin while in its presence, the Tarahumara worshipped *hikuli* (peyote) as a deity, praising it for its "beautiful intoxication."

Lumholtz also encountered *hikuritamete* or "peyote hunters" from the nearby Huichol or Wixárika tribe. For the Huichol, the peyote cactus, along with cevidae (deer) and maize, occupies a hypostatic position in a Southwestern answer to the Holy Trinity. This tribal trio forms the tripartite backbone of Huichol ritual and belief, and without any one of those three constituents, the other two would surely disappear, too. For without shedding the blood of the deer, the sun will not cause the maize to grow. But things must be done in the right order. It is imperative that the deer should not be offered prior to the peyote hunt. Moreover, the ceremony of parching the maize (similar to the preparation of popcorn), which is believed to bring the rains necessary to produce the next crop, cannot be held without the presence of *hikuri*. And the hikuri mustn't be harvested until after the maize has been purged and sanctified.[10] These three supports form an indivisible complex on which the entire Huichol way of life is balanced. Donning colorful ceremonial attire, temporarily adopting a special liturgical language, the Huichol would trek over two thousand kilometers, year after year, into the mesas found high above Real de Catorce and onto the holy hunting ground known as *Wirikuta*. Once there, entering what Romanian historian of religion Mircea Eliade referred to as *in illo tempore* (mythical time), the Wixárika would reenact the myth of hikuri and *el venado azul*—the sacred blue deer, named Kauyumari—whose magical self-sacrifice brought peyote to the people.

The elderly told us that long time ago, high in the Huichol mountains, the grandparents reunited to discuss about their situation. Their people was sick, there was no water or food, it wasn't raining and land was dry. They decided to send four young men hunting, with the mission of bringing back any food that they were able to obtain to share them with the community, it didn't matter if it was little or a lot . . .

Next morning, the young men started their journey, each one of them armed with their bow and arrows. They walked for days, until one afternoon, something jumped behind the bushes, it was a big fat deer. The young men were exhausted and hungry, but when they saw the deer, they forgot about everything and started running after it. The deer looked at them and felt compassion. He left them rest that night and next morning prompted to continue the hunting.

Many weeks passed by before arriving to Wirikuta . . . When the young men were walking on the hill, near the Narices hill, they saw the deer jumping in direction of where the Earth Spirit lives. They could swear they saw the deer running in that direction, and tried to find him without success. Suddenly, one of the men shot an arrow that fell inside a deer figure formed by peyote plants, that under the sun, they shined like emeralds do.

The young men were confused by what had just happened, but decided to cut the plants in shape of a Marratutuyari (deer) to take them to the village. After walking during several days, they arrived to the Huichol mountain, where everyone was waiting. Walking straight to the old men, they told them their experience. The elderly started to distribute peyote to the community, and after a while, they were no longer hungry or thirsty.

Ever since, Huichols adore peyote, which at the same time is deer and corn, a guiding spirit. And every year, they continue walking from the Huichol mountains to Wirikuta, keeping that same route alive, to pray God for rain, food and health for their people. (As told by Enrique Alejos, Cultural Concierge of the Four Seasons Resort Punta Mita.)

Upon their departure for Wirikuta, like Alice through the looking glass, the Wixárika pilgrims would progressively enter into a topsy-turvy world, where everything acquired the qualities of its antithesis—up became down, left became right, yes became no, and so on. Moreover, labor divisions and hierarchy were switched, things of beauty derided as objects of disgust, and those enwrapped in conversation did so back-to-back, all the while employing the opposites of words usually demanded by common discourse. Furthermore, each day of the journey, the mara'akáme (a Huichol shaman) would add new reversals to the lingo that the entire troupe had to adopt and keep up with for the duration of the peyote pilgrimage. Long before the ritual consumption of the cactus itself, therefore, each of the Wixárika would have already been well on his way into a profound altered state of consciousness (ASC). Like Carnivàle among Christians and Purim for those of Jewish descent, to embark upon the sacred pilgrimage to Wirikuta was, for the Huichol Natives, quite literally to be transported into another world.[11]

Around the same time that Lumholtz was interacting with the Tarahumara and the Wixárika, whose implicit relationships with the peyote cactus are said to reach back untold eons, a man named James Mooney, of the Smithsonian Institution's Bureau of Ethnology, was being invited by a young Kiowa tribesman to attend a secretive ceremony, high in the Ouachita, where *seni*—peyote—was being ritually consumed. While he himself did not participate, the eager ethnologist did acquiesce. What Mooney observed on that fateful evening, in a riverside tipi shared by Kiowas, Comanches, and Apaches alike, were the beginning stages of the emerging "Half Moon" ceremony—the central rite of what would soon come to be known as the Native American Church.[12] Although it had officially spread to what were once Caddoan lands located in the Southeast (in Oklahoma), the ceremonial use of the peyote cactus in that part of the continent was a fairly recent phenomenon, allegedly dating back no further than the nineteenth century. But throughout this book we're going to learn that the Natives of the Southeastern Ceremonial Complex, long before the arrival of *Lophophora williamsii*, were already possessed of their own multifaceted, rich entheogenic traditions.

For the sake of completeness, three additional shamanic substances known to the Americas are worth briefly mentioning here: "mescal beans," cacao, and alcohol. There being less to say in regard to it, I shall begin with mescal beans.

Not to be confused with alcoholic agave concoctions or "mescalito" (peyote), another archaic hallucinogen employed in ancient North America—although far less well known—were the brilliant red seeds of *Sophora secundiflora*—aka the highly toxic "mescal bean." Still used in the construction of Native American jewelry in the Southwest, mescal beans are rarely, if ever, used today in an entheogenic context due to the presence of the poisonous alkaloid cystine. Pharmacologically, cystine is closely related to nicotine, although mescal beans differ from tobacco in that they are exceedingly dangerous to work with, having effects that include the induction of severe nausea, convulsions, and, at higher doses, death due to respiratory failure. Even so, along with preserved peyote specimens and Mexican horse chestnuts (*Ungnadia speciosa*), deposits of mescal beans have been recovered from ritual caves dating back as far as eight thousand years. Half of a bean is said to be sufficient to induce a pronounced state of delirium that can persist for up to seventy-two hours.[13] Like alcohol, *Sophora secundiflora* is mentioned here only for the sake of being comprehensive, but the delirium it induces was indeed once a highly sought-after shamanic tool. However, its use has been almost totally eclipsed by the comparably safer tobacco and by the more reliable peyote cactus.[14]

The use of cacao (*Theobroma cacao*) as an inebriant and as a ritual substance is thought to be extremely ancient in Central and South America. Originally domesticated some five thousand years ago in and around Iquitos in modern day Peru and Ecuador, cacao eventually spread into North America[15]—with the beans reaching even the Ancestral Puebloans in Chaco Canyon, some 1,900 kilometers away. Indeed, in Room 28 of Pueblo Bonito, archaeologists discovered at least 112 cylinder jars, remarkably similar to those used ceremonially to imbibe cacao farther south, that were found to contain residues of theobromine—a sure sign that cacao was being employed in northwestern New Mexico, possibly as early as the tenth century.[16]

Among the Aztecs, cacao was believed to be a gift from the god Quetzalcoatl, a peaceful, plumed serpent—not to be confused, however, with the Great Serpent of the MIIS, which is often also shown as being possessed of wings. When consumed green or unripe, cacao can have strong inebriating properties. It is no surprise, then, that it was historically used in conjunction with psilocybin "magic" mushrooms, such as *Psilocybe mexicana*—also said to be a gift from the god.[17] According to the Zapotecs and Mazatecs, wherever Quetzalcoatl's blood fell to the ground, from that spot sprouted psychedelic mushrooms.[18] Both an offering and a medicine, cacao could also be incinerated upon charcoal for the purpose of fumigation. In Panama, for instance, along with the pods of certain sacred chilis (*Capsicum frutescens*), the Cuna Indians would burn cacao beans as a form of healing incense.[19]

Perhaps surprisingly, alcohol, too, found its way into various ceremonial and social settings of Indigenous Americans. While distilled liquors did not enter the sphere of the Amerindian until after the arrival of the Spanish and other European colonists, lightly fermented "beers" and "wines" were well known to certain Native peoples, at least during the Mississippian Period[20]—albeit mostly limited to the Natives of the Southwest. Ranging from roughly 8–14 percent ABV,[21] these slightly inebriating Southwestern concoctions were prepared primarily from varieties of cacti, including saguaro, agave, prickly pear, and pitaya, from succulents such as aloe, and from sprouted grains like maize.[22] Gas chromatography analysis of Pueblo Bonito potsherds from Chaco Canyon, dating back some twelve hundred years, for instance, shows that Puebloans were fermenting kernels of maize to produce a gentle, alcoholic brew as early as the ninth century.[23] The few examples known from the Southeast, on the other hand, come to us mainly from the Georgia Creeks and Cherokee of the Carolinas, both of whom who used fermented berries and fruit to produce their own wine-like beverages.[24] Unlike the recreational application of alcoholic drinks familiar in the modern West, even this minimalistic use among Native Americans appears to have been strictly limited to sacred shamanic and ceremonial settings.[25]

With the arrival of the Spanish and French, though, this traditional usage was expanded to include the far more detrimental distilled spirits, such as whiskey, rum, and brandy. In many instances, this intoxicating innovation proved a welcome addition to an already potent repertoire of ritual substances. As early as 1680, the use of liquor among an Algonquian settlement in Govanus (present-day Brooklyn) was documented by a pair of Dutch Labadists, who described what was clearly a shamanic healing session. The Ojibwa were also in the practice of using liquor—as both a tool for divination and as an offering to the Manitou spirits—while the Naskapi-Montagnais relied on alcoholic drink for the induction of prophetic, omened dreams. For the Central Algonquians, liquor found an important place in mourning and mortuary practices, while the Delawares used it in more life-affirming and social contexts, such as sharing and gift giving—a deliberate show of hospitality and group solidarity.[26] In my personal opinion, these anecdotes regarding the use of "beer," "wine," and even spirits within the ceremonies of certain Indigenous peoples speak to both the ingenuity and the adaptability of the Amerindians. At the same time, it is important information in that it works to dispel the fallacious myth of what has been dubbed the "firewater" fairy tale—that Europeans are genetically predisposed toward drinking, while Native Americans are alleged to be the opposite.[27]

In the context of Central Algonquian shamanism in particular, liquor became an essential ingredient in the rites of the Wabeno, the Jessakid, and even the Midéwiwin. Similar to the "Grand Medicine Society," the Wabeno were a sodality of shamanic healers whose specialty was the construction of sacred, magical powders designed to assist clients in important personal matters—such as the acquisition of love and success in hunts. Around 1800, the American superintendent of Indian Affairs reported a request for the provision of whiskey at Wabeno rites: "Friend, friend, whiskey for the wabana," was the magicians' gentle plea. The often-feared Jessakid, infamous for their theatrical "shaking tent" rituals in which disembodied spirits, as well as the souls of living men, could be conjured, threatened, restrained, and even killed, also regularly employed strong drink in their performance: "The devils were thirsty, and wanted something to drink," relayed Thomas McKenney, head of the U.S. Bureau of Indian Affairs in the War Department, in 1826. According to the report of Canadian anthropologist Diamond Jenness over a century later, the conjurer's spirit helpers consumed tobacco and whiskey, alongside the Jessakid himself, while in the shaking tent. The whiskey was therefore required "partly to pour libations to the gods, and partly to drink in order that he may acquire the proper frenzy." This intoxicating trend continued with the rites of the Midéwiwin or "Grand Medicine Society." In 1804, a fur trader named Thomas Conner, for instance, was asked for rum by a number of Ojibwa Natives, for "to make their Mittay Ceremony." Another trader, in 1820, recorded similarly: "all the Indians Dancing, the House [Midewiwin lodge] contains near 160. They kept it up till sun set [. . .] & drank 1 ½ keg Rum. . ." Finally, in 1817, the Canadian superintendent of Indian Service noted of the Potawatomi that "their chief needed some rum to make a Metaiway (Medewiwin) feast."[28]

Typical of shamanic practice, liquor was also prized as a trusted mode of medical diagnosis. It is understandably difficult for a modern Westerner to imagine a scenario wherein one's health care professional must rely on a good alcohol buzz to properly diagnose a physical malady. It must be borne in mind, however, that, for many Indigenous healers, bodily ailments are merely the byproduct of a much more fundamental metaphysical affliction. Moreover, a healer's direct perception of those supernatural hindrances was largely dependent upon the attainment of an altered state of consciousness. This was certainly the case with Penobscot guide Joe Polis, a self-described Indian "doctor." Canoeing with American transcendentalist Henry David Thoreau through the Maine wilderness, Polis unexpectedly fell ill and requested a bottle of brandy of Thoreau—not as a viable treatment for the illness, but to establish contact with the spirits—thereby enabling him to assess the ailment and affect a prognosis. "Me doctor," said the Penobscot healer. "First study my case, find out what ail 'em," he added, "then I know what to take."[29] As effective as alcohol appears to have been in this regard, there are nonetheless far more potent entheogenic substances to which Native Americans had recourse to diagnose—and treat—illness.

A syrupy tea known as black drink, prepared using the caffeine-rich leaves of *cassina*—a species of yaupon holly (*Ilex vomitoria*) and a close cousin of South America's yerba-maté—was also used extensively by the Southeastern Ceremonial Complex. However, insofar as this ritual substance figures largely in our later discussions, we will refrain from giving it treatment here.

In the pages that follow, we are going to visit some of the key mound complexes of the Mississippian Ideological Interaction Sphere— including Cahokia, Spiro, Etowah, and Moundville—before performing a survey of the entheogenic contents of various botanical assemblages recovered from those sites. We're also going to take a close look at some telling organic residues found on effigy and mortuary pottery, marine-shell medicine cups, and flint clay pipes. Finally, we'll take a close look at the possibility that "magic" mushrooms, and even a local form of ayahuasca, were being used by the Mississippians. The findings may surprise you. Nevertheless, rather than barge in unannounced on an already bustling, busy complex like Cahokia or Spiro, let us first begin our journey just a little farther northwest, on the opposite side of the Mississippi River, in an animated, colorful cave located somewhere on private property in Warren County, Missouri. For it is in the depths of the dark zone of Picture Cave that the Mississippian culture may be said to have been first conceived.

TWO

A CAVERN OF SACRED VISIONS

To the twenty-first-century mind, the cave readily invokes negative notions of the primitive and the bestial. The very word *troglodyte*, moreover (even though evidence suggests that none of these places ever served as long-term habitations), conjures up the crudest of conceptualizations, usually including unflattering adjectives such as *barbarous*, *unevolved*, *rudimentary*, and the favorite pejorative of the learned ethnographers of the nineteenth century, *savage*. In the Indigenous mind, however, the insulation of the stony grotto, with its deep, damp darkness, was instead imagined more as a cavernous, fertile womb. Indeed, this is especially true of moist karst or solutional caves—the kind containing those fantastic fluidlike formations—which are literally considered "living" insofar as they actually breathe, change, and grow, developing slowly over long periods of time. Because of the oftentimes acidic nature of the water in these regions, at a rate of potentially six or seven ounces per day—roughly the size of a softball—karst cave walls are continuously carved out by cascades and currents of water. This relentless aquatic activity scoops and sculpts the malleable marble and liquefies limestone into sometimes complex systems of tunnel-like caverns that can stretch for miles beneath the surface of the earth. In fact, geologists have determined that cave passages harboring active rivers or streams can grow upward of one millimeter per year—that's roughly a meter or more of fresh growth for every thousand years.[1]

While that doesn't sound like much, it adds up. Kentucky's Mammoth Cave, for example, the longest known cave system in the world, goes on for almost 725 kilometers with Mammoth Dome arching at a height of 58.5 meters and the Bottomless Pit at 32 meters deep. This means that, by the above calculations, Mammoth Cave alone has been actively growing for around 692,018,000 years. Ergo, not only can it be said that some caves are essentially *alive*, but for all practical purposes, they're also basically immortal.

Is it any wonder, then, that several Native American tribes have purported that when their people first emerged from inside the earth, they did so out of the mouths of caves? The Chickasaw, Creek, and Choctaw, for instance, hold a belief that when the Great Creator fashioned the First Peoples, he did so inside of an ancient platform mound. This site, located in Winston County, Mississippi, is called by the Natives *Nanih Waiya*, meaning "Leaning Hill," and constitutes their *Inholitopa iski* or Mother Mound. Shortly after the peoples' formation, it is said that the newly created human beings were then born from nearby Nanih Waiya Cave, lying roughly 1.5 kilometers east, in Neshoba County. Only recently, as of 2008, has the Mississippi Band of Choctaw Indians regained control of these important ancestral sites. Similarly, the Lakota or Dakota, also known as the Teton Sioux, claim to have emerged from a sacred cave in Custer County, South Dakota—called by them *Washun Niya*, "Wind Cave." In 1903, President Theodore Roosevelt designated it a national park, making Wind Cave the sixth national park in the United States—and the first cave in the world to be named as such. A little farther west, located in the Grand Canyon, on the Little Colorado River, is a breathtaking glacier-ice-blue travertine dome and spring, known under the Hopi name *Sipapu*—loosely translated as "Place of Emergence"—which is claimed as the birthplace of at least three neighboring Native American tribes: the Hopi, the Navajo, and the Zuni. Interestingly, in commemoration of this creation myth, a little hole or bowl-shaped depression is made in the floor of every *kiva*—a small, subterranean, circular "pithouse," crafted by Puebloans prior to 1250 CE for the private practice of ceremonies and politics—that takes its name

from this ancestral Place of Emergence. Also, although there's no ethnographic literature to support the claims, Mezcal Mountain in Sedona is
even equipped with a natural feature known as the Birthing Cave, allegedly used by Hopi women who were awaiting labor. Thus, to the ancient
Amerindian, caves could acquire qualities both creative and maternal.
Although, as with any authentic archetype, in the ingenious Indigenous
intellect the imago of the cave is also prone to enantiodromia—that is,
to transforming autonomously from a metaphorical womb into a very
real tomb. In such cases, the mouth of the cavern has been unconsciously
converted into a veritable liminal threshold, leading prehistoric spelunkers directly into the Underworld below.

Therefore, for many Indigenous Americans, caves could also carry
an admittedly graver air. In some such cases, Natives were wont to
deposit the remains of their deceased deep inside of mortuary caves. The
reasoning behind choosing a cavern as a final resting place—as opposed
to the more common burial ground or mound—may seem obscure. But
what is a mound but a manmade cave? I'll cite a few examples. The
aforementioned Mammoth Cave in Kentucky, for instance, housed the
desiccated remains of at least two ancient humans—albeit only one that
was actually a proper, intentional burial (the other being the remains
of a rather unfortunate individual who accidentally met his end while
harvesting gypsum).[2] A third mummified individual, known as Fawn
Hoof, was billed to tourists as having been found in Mammoth Cave,
although it is likely that he was in reality the second of a pair of burials discovered in Short Cave—also located in the Bluegrass State. The
other of the two Short Cave interments was a small child who had been
carefully enveloped in the hide of a deer. Unfortunately, upon exposure
to the moisture of the open air, within the space of a few hours the
remains crumbled "into its natural dust."[3]

The extremely dry conditions of the nitrate-rich caverns of
Appalachia, and especially the Cumberland Plateau, lent themselves to
the remarkable preservation of human remains as well as their accompanying mortuary artifacts—such as cordage, weavings, basketry, feathers, and animal skins. In point of fact, it was a group of nitrate miners,

exploiting a cave in Warren County, Tennessee, in search of resources required for the production of gunpowder, who stumbled upon another pair of mummified Natives.

> [In Big Bone Cave,] at about six feet below the surface of the cave, something like clothing was discovered, which, upon proper examination, was found to be the shrouding of some dead bodies. Upon further investigation, the bodies were found to be two in number, a male and female, which [. . .] they judged to have been buried in ancient times. [. . .] They supposed the male to have been at the time of his decease around 25 years of age. He was enveloped in the following manner: first, with a fine linen shirt. His legs were drawn up, then five deer skins were closely bound round his body. A twilled blanket, wrapped around them, and a cane mat sixty feet long, wrapped round the whole. His frame was entire except for the bowels; his hair, of a fair complexion; his teeth, remarkably sound; his stature, above the common. The body of the female was found interred about three feet from that of the other. Its position of lying was similar to that of the male. The carcase was enveloped first with two undressed deer skins, under which, upon the face, was found a small cane mat. Then four dressed deer skins were wrapped round it, over which was folded a cane mat large enough to cover the whole. There were then five sheets, supposed to be made of nettle lint, wrought up curiously around each side with feathers of various kinds and colours. Two fans of feathers were found next, upon the breast. The body, with the whole of the before described wrapping, was found on what was believed to be a hair trunk or box, with a cane cover, which was wound up in two well-dressed deerskins of the largest kind; the whole girthed with two straps: the female is supposed to have been from 12 to 15 years of age: her hair short and black; the body entire; the eyes as full and prominent as if alive.[4]

Carbon dating on a single woven fiber bag discovered in the same Tennessee cave has placed these desiccated remains firmly within the

Middle Woodland Period. In a different Tennessee cave, two more burials, having an almost identical setting, were found by a different group of nitrate miners.

> In digging for saltpeter in 1811, on Dutch River, Smith Co. Tennessee, a large stone was discovered across the mouth of a cave. On entering the cave, which appeared natural in the limestone rock, resembled a vault or ancient sepulcher, the bodies of two human persons were discovered. They were male and female, and each in a curious wrought basket made of splits of cane. The bodies were in a sitting posture. Around each body was wrapped a kind of large shroud [?] or plaid [?] seemingly wrought with the fingers and made of the best matting resembling wild nettles or Indian hemp.[5]

Not all mortuary caves were prepared in this primal way, however. In a discovery reported in the Tennessee newspaper *Nashville Union* in 1885, for example, a man named J. R. Stubblefield stumbled upon a stunning sight. A curious cavern in Grundy County housed "at least 20 skulls all touching each other, besides which was a bed of bones beneath and around them of all parts of the human skeleton." Above the bones were painted, in ocher, a series of vermilion dots—possibly a dating or numbering system, similar to the recent hypothesis proposed by a team of researchers in an early 2023 paper, published online by Cambridge University Press, titled "An Upper Palaeolithic Proto-Writing System and Phenological Calendar."[6] Suggestive of the Woodland Period, this interment differed from those previously discussed in that the rustic animal skins and woven textiles were replaced by delicate mica sheets, mineral ore, one single bead, several projectile points, a pipe stone, polished stones, and an individual piece of copper. Roughly 170 kilometers north, in Pickett County, was found a similar Woodland Period scene—albeit a burial concealing a much larger cache of artifacts. Among the remains of Native Americans resting upon the floor of this sealed vault were recovered a number of pipes, shell gorgets, pottery bowls and other ceramic vessels, thousands of shell beads, and grave goods prepared from various animal bones.[7]

Approaching the Mississippian Period proper, Tennessee archaeologist E. F. Hassler reported in 1946, in an unnamed cavern in the northern portion of the state, a strikingly different, highly organized pattern—described by him as "the most spectacular cave in this immediate region." Placed in anatomically correct positions were no less than thirty complete skeletons, all of which "had been deposited near the right-hand and left-hand walls at right angles to them and with heads next to the walls." "Burial accompaniments were mostly in the form of shell beads and ornaments," Hassler reported, "although a few stone objects were present." Complex cave discoveries of this kind continued with a series of burials in the Copena cave in Alabama, this time containing "wooden grave furniture, mica, galena, and other exotic grave goods."[8] And the list goes on.

Naturally, it is in this chthonic, Below World capacity that a number of archaic, artistically embellished caverns, such as the profusely illustrated Picture Cave in Missouri, came to serve as liminal locales for intensive, isolated psychedelic rites.[9] I use the word *psychedelic* here in its literal, definitive sense: *psyche*, "soul," and *dēlein*, "to manifest." For caves have long been associated with shamanic practice involving the ritual use of entheogenic plants.[10] In fact, it has been proposed that, based on a comprehensive study of over forty thousand years' worth of cave paintings and petroglyphs, the inspiration behind the geometric designs—known as form constants—repeatedly discovered in prehistoric cave dwellings and sacred sites was very likely hallucinogenic drugs.[11] It is a well-known trope that, with or without the use of psychedelic drugs, sensory deprivation of the sort experienced during prolonged isolation is sufficient to induce significant changes in one's perception and mental state. And alteration of consciousness is the very laudable pursuit for which shamans and seers, since time immemorial, have retreated, deaf and blind, into the subterranean depths of sacred caverns.[12] Further, it is worth noting that the "light-at-the-end-of-the-tunnel" effect of emerging from an extended cavern retreat is possessed of an obvious yet impactful correlation to classic reports of near-death experiences.[13] Their ceremonial and symbolic applications may be truly immense. That doesn't mean that there were no psychedelic spelunkers, though. The privacy provided by underground caverns made them sought-out, choice locations for ritualized retreats like ceremonial psychedelic sessions. Prime examples of such inspired usage are the six-thousand-year-old apian Tassili Mushroom Figure, commonly referred to as the "bee-faced mushroom shaman," or "bee-headed shaman," found in a cave in Tassili n'Ajjer and the equally aged Selva Pascuala cave mural in Spain—the latter of which depicts a number of fruiting bodies that ethnomycologists have identified as the psychedelic, coprophilous *Psilocybe hispanica* mushroom. Another great example is the exquisitely executed ocher datura spirals found decorating the walls of California's Pinwheel Cave—to which we'll return in chapter seven. Indeed, perhaps more than any other natural formation, caverns were universal in their appeal as sacred spaces, inviting shamans and ritualists to explore their depths in search of otherworldly encounters accessible through trance.

Within the hallowed hollows of Missouri's Picture Cave, Indigenous Americans—some having traveled from at least 160 kilometers away—sequestered themselves deep inside the inky insulation of the soundless dark zones. Fasting, patiently awaiting the visual manifestation of celestial or subterranean nonhuman entities, questing querents would inquisitively stare into the vast and endless silent darkness. From out of this abysmal midnight canvas, like a dream emerging from the backdrop of sleep, fantastic forms and impossible images would at first seem to flicker, then materialize, as if emerging ex nihilo: stately hominids with long-nosed faces where their ears should be . . . furry, ferocious beasts having plated, segmented, insect-like tails . . . disembodied arms reaching down from the ceiling, with horned bison heads in place of their hands. . . . Once the visionary experience had been attained, the revelatory content was then faithfully recorded upon the blank field of the cavern walls. As one might expect, many of these same surreal subjects have been abstracted from their ethereal environments and impressively immortalized upon the panels of Picture Cave. Between two distinct caverns and a dozen separate panels, Picture Cave boasts no fewer than 294 cogent pic-

◎ ◎ ◎

Fig. 2.1. Disembodied arm, draped with an otter skin pouch, reaching down from the ceiling of Picture Cave, showing a horned bison in place of a hand.

Photo by the author

tographs, depicting practically everything under (and including) the sun, from humanoid warriors, quadrupedal beasts, and majestic raptors, to slithering serpents, abstract "phantasmagoria," and a mortifying motif known in archaeological circles by the very technical term *toothy mouths*.[14] It is my suspicion, however, that, at least in a few cases, some of these "toothy mouths" may in fact be depictions of cowrie or mégis shells. Indeed, the association between these magical Midé amulets and the Below World supernatural who gifted the sacred bundles of the Midéwiwin to the Anishinaabe was so strong, in fact, that members of the Grand Medicine Society often refer to the latter affectionately as simply "Shell." Moreover, with its characteristic, jagged orifice, the open underside of the cowrie—generally held *in the mouth* of the candidate or patient during Midé rites—resembles nothing so much as a toothy mouth.*

Here, in the darkness of a remote cavern in eastern Missouri, literally located in the middle of nowhere, the seeds of the great Mississippian culture first began to take root. In Picture Cave, for perhaps the first time ever, we as an audience are introduced visually to a number of important nonhuman personas, such as Horned Serpent, Underwater Panther, Raptor on the Path, and so on, that are going to figure prominently in the Path of Souls cycle as the same is encountered in the MIIS. In fact, as you're about to see, Picture Cave is not unlike a microcosmic fractal, reiterating the entire demographic of the Mississippian Art and Ceremonial Complex in compact form. For instance, the dominant themes found painted on the walls of Picture Cave 1 (PC1) and Picture Cave 2 (PC2) are divided comparably to that seen in regard to the economy of images maintained between Cahokia on the one hand and the necropolis of Moundville in the south on the other. In PC1, just like at Cahokia,[16] celestial figures such as *avimorphs* appear to dominate the scene.[17] Meanwhile, in PC2, just as in Moundville, chthonic Lower World motifs like *herpetomorphs* are prevalent.[18] The Hemphill Winged Serpent is found nowhere else but in the confines of Moundville, while the Classic Braden–style "Birdman" is completely absent from Alabama—being local instead to Cahokia.[19] Conceivably, the Mississippian conceptualization of the cosmos is organized according to this same naturalistic three-tiered pattern,[20] with avimorphs ruling the Above World, herpetomorphs controlling the Below, and *anthropomorphs* and quadrupeds sandwiched firmly in between. Depending on the class of supernatural

---

*Why they were placed in the mouth is not entirely clear—although Hoffman does note that certain drugs appear to have been administered at some point during the ritual. Psychedelics having been unknown at the time (mescaline wasn't discovered until six years after the publication of *Midē'wiwin*), the author speculates that strychnia, a poison originating from *Strychnos nux-vomica*, may have been employed.[15] However, insofar as the strychnine tree is native to India and Southeast Asia, and therefore would have had to have been introduced to the New World by the British, strychnine cannot account for the action in pre-Columbian times.

⊙ ⊙ ⊙

Fig. 2.2. A depiction of a death rite, found in Picture Cave,
officiated by a shaman dressed as a bird. See also color plate 5.

Photo by the author

that the individual intended to invoke, courageous questers could ritually retire to PC1 or PC2 and calmly await expedient responses to their pressing, perfervid calls.[21]

In addition to portraits of preternatural persons, Picture Cave also depicts apparently common individuals—albeit engaged in decidedly uncommon behaviors—that may give us an idea as to the variety of rituals reserved for this site. One such glyph worth mentioning even shows what appears to be a magical rite of death and resurrection[22]—ostensibly a type of shamanic initiation—not unlike that practiced by the mystical and mysterious Midéwiwin, better known as the Midé or Grand Medicine Society of Ontario, Manitoba, Wisconsin, and Minnesota.[23] A nearly identical rite was also known to the Dhegihan people in the form of their magical Shell Society. The inclusion of this "raising" scene among the glyphs at Picture Cave should thus be taken as a good indication that such or similar rites were indeed practiced there.

Moreover, the Midéwiwin, while traditionally styled a medicine society, were responsible for guarding and controlling the secretive, initiatory wisdom that constitutes the topography of the Path of Souls. It is said of members of the fourth and final degree that they have acquired the power to affect life and death. This belief is reflected in the initiation rituals of the Midéwiwin themselves. In each successive grade, for instance, induction into the society involved the ceremonial "shooting"—*spitting* would be closer to the mark—of magical mégis shells (i.e., cowries) into the very bodies of advancing candidates. The heart-like, Reuleaux triangle–shaped object depicted in the left hand of one of the two "ritualists" shown in Picture Cave may answer to just such a ceremonial tool. Indeed, on at least two occasions, in the *wiigwaasabakoon*—sacred birch-bark scrolls—of the Midéwiwin, a heart is substituted for the mégis.[24] When it is portrayed in the grip of an anthropomorphic figure (such as a shaman), it is not uncommon to see mégis shells represented as being at least as large as the "shaman's" hand. And, if the mégis is drawn without its characteristic rays, dots, or cross-hatching, it can be next to impossible to distinguish it from an artistic illustration of a shaman's drum.[25] At the climactic point in the Midé rite at which the mégis shells are "shot" at the individuals, the bodies of the inductees would lifelessly drop to the earthen ground—and there they would lie, completely motionless, as though they'd been killed by the mysterious potency of the mégis. It is only with the aid of their miraculous *pinji'gosân* or animal pelt pouches (containing healing herbs and sacred shells), also called a *midéwayan*, that the attending Midé are able to raise the novices from their death-like trance. In fact, one such medicine sack appears to be draped over the left of the two enormous, disembodied arms, descending from the ceiling of Picture Cave (described above). Furthermore, under certain special circumstances, a Midé Lodge could assume the guise of something known as a *Dzhibai' Midéwigân*—a "Ghost Lodge." In this grave capacity, members of the sodality took on the roles of psychopompic guides—leading the spirits of the recently deceased safely along the Path of Souls.[26]

To the Indigenous mind, caves could take on a number of metaphorical characteristics. Possessed of the qualities of both womb and tomb, Picture Cave was a liminal space where Indigenous ritualists and Native vision questers, traveling from perhaps hundreds of miles around, could retreat to ceremoniously die to themselves before undergoing a rebirth from the ashes of their own being. But just how was such a spiritual crisis orchestrated or created? In the case of the recently deceased, obviously it is the reality of their own demise that has propelled them into the afterlife state. However, regarding those still-living sorcerers who, commanding power over life and death, officiate the ritual initiations of others—symbolically killing and raising them from the dead while instructing the novices in the secret wisdom—how were they able to traverse a causeway that is intended solely for the footfall of the dead? Well, I shall tell you. They did so in the same way that the tobacco shamans (discussed above) did it—with the aid of entheogenic plants.[27]

THREE

A FINGER POINTING AT THE CAHOKIA MOON

If Picture Cave constitutes the conception of the Mississippian culture, then Cahokia surely comprises its birth. Like Picture Cave, Cahokia was part of the region archaeologists refer to as the Middle Mississippian culture. Compared to other MIIS-related complexes, Cahokia is curious in the extreme. As opposed to being plotted on a cardinal axis, Cahokia was instead oriented exactly five degrees east of true north. As you're about to learn, by placing the city on an off-center grid, Cahokia was precisely positioned to point at both the northern and southern maximum moonrises and the sunrise and sunset of the summer and winter solstices, respectively.[1] Participating therefore in both solar and lunar cycles, Cahokia amounted to a very special city indeed. It was mainly the moon, however, that occupied the attention of the Cahokians. You're about to see why.

The plan for Cahokia's main precinct is similar to the layout we just saw in Picture Cave—and to the entire Mississippian world, as we'll learn below—with the mountainous and celestial Monk's Mound anchoring one end of the city to the skies and the infernal, muggy Rattlesnake Mound tying the opposite side to the netherworld below. That is, the vertical dimension was also represented on the horizontal plane, built into the location's layout. Moreover, not unlike the serpentine supernatural that must be coaxed into stretching himself across the aquatic chasm on the Path of Souls in the form of a fallen tree trunk uniting the two embankments (p. 7), bridging Monk's Mound and the Rattlesnake Mound is a remarkably straight, kilometer-long viaduct, elevated well above and crossing Cahokia's marshy floodplain. Eighteen meters wide, this unswerving overpass, known as the Rattlesnake Causeway, ultimately amounts to an access road approaching the afterlife. For the oval-shaped Rattlesnake Mound—named so on account of the rattlesnakes that are known to congregate there during flood months (whose markings bear a remarkable similarity to the vulvar shape of the ogee)—is a ridge-top mound that functioned as a terrestrial ogee, similar to the celestial ogee observable in the constellation of the Hand— Messier 42, or the Orion Nebula, to be exact. However, where Mississippian cities to the south—Moundville, for example—focused on the southern portal, accessible on or near the winter solstice, Cahokians favored the northern portal, accessible in the summer.[2] In point of fact, on the summer solstice the northern pole of the Milky Way sits directly atop the Rattlesnake Mound, like a pot of gold at the end of a rainbow. Following the Rattlesnake Causeway to this ovular ogee, the impression one gets from observing the perspective is that the pathway does not end at Rattlesnake Mound but makes a sharp turn upward in one continuous movement, leading the soul into the Above World in the sky. Cahokia, therefore, constituted a complete microcosm in itself.

Vertically, Monk's Mound occupies the central position of axis mundi, bridging the three separate tiers of the Mississippian cosmos—Below, Middle, and Above.[3] Regularly represented by a pole or tree, a column of smoke, or even a mound, mountain, or pyramid, the axis mundi constitutes a universal concept among Indigenous Americans. It is understood to serve as the interface betwixt the horizontal plane of the earthly and mundane—here signified by an equal-arm crux encoded in Cahokia's quaternity of plazas, connected to the cardinal directions, solstices, and equinoxes—and the vertical dimension of the transmundane, bridging the Indigenous equivalent of heaven and Hades with the Middle World. Rising up and out of the swamp-like floodplain, rooted deep in the Below World underneath,

Monk's Mound towers some thirty meters high, scraping against the starry skyscape, like a manufactured holy mountain. For that is exactly what it was built to be. Surrounding this central "point," creating an undeniable, distinctive cruciform design, are four large, wide-open plazas, like petals around a dogwood flower, where people from all over the precinct would gather for various public activities, such as, perhaps, feasting, crafting, and playing the game of chunkey.[4] Although we will detect this same crux implied in the schema of Craig Mound at Spiro and Mound C at Etowah, archaeologists have argued that this geometrical configuration at Cahokia was an intentional attempt to encode certain specific astrological phenomena—namely, a stellar cross created by the intersection of perpendicular lines formed from Betelgeuse and Rigel on the west-east arm and the three stars comprising Orion's belt, known by the Osage as the sign of the Three Deer, on the north-south arm—into the terrestrial landscape of Cahokia.[5] I'm willing to take this one step further and say that the main precinct of the city of Cahokia may have been deliberately built to reflect many, if not all, of the visible stars surrounding the Osage sign of the Three Deer. Working from that reference point resulted in a complex, anthropomorphic configuration of plots that most modern Westerners would immediately recognize as the constellation of Orion. Thus, even though evidence has shown that Cahokian elites were prone to exploit the northern gate to the Milky Way in and around the summer solstice, it is clear from the city's topography that the section of the sky surrounding the Chief's Hand constellation also held great significance for those who designed the site. We have already shown in the introduction why this southern section of stars was the focus of so much of Cahokia's attention: it is the location of the ogee, one of the entrance points leading the dead onto the Path of Souls.

There are a number of reasons why Cahokia and Picture Cave are seen by some archaeologists as being related. In addition to reports of "Cahokia points" recovered from the site,[6] some of the artwork in Picture Cave, such as the Pinocchioesque "long-nosed maskettes" or

◎ ◎ ◎

Fig. 3.1. Red Horn or Morning Star, as he appears in Picture Cave. See also color plate 6.
Photo by the author

the so-called ghostly "Black Warrior" glyph, for example, is clearly executed in the Early Classic Braden style—a genre of aesthetics centered on realistic representation and traceable to the early expansion period at Cahokia.[7] Prior to that early expansion, Native Americans in the Eastern Woodlands are believed to have existed primarily in small, migratory clusters, periodically convening on sacred sites marked by the erection of burial mounds and earthworks. Traveling north or south as the seasons shifted, Indigenous tribes seem to have been forever relocating as resources and weather fluctuated throughout the months and years. Archaeological evidence shows that entire areas would be repeatedly occupied and abandoned, only to be resettled, year after year—with the occasional decade- or even centuries-long desertion. However, all of a sudden and without warning, between the beginning of the tenth century and midway through the eleventh, Cahokia's meager population unexpectedly exploded, expanding from around two thousand inhabitants to close to twenty thousand permanent citizens. Obviously, that's an enormous enlargement. How did it happen? What sorts of environmental, religious, or political alterations would need to take place to enable an extreme magnification of populace on the scale evidenced at Cahokia? Let's take a moment to look at some of the major changes that occurred during its early expansion period and consider some of the potential factors that may have contributed to the unexpected ballooning of Cahokia's population.

CAHOKIA'S CLIMATE

Perhaps the most obvious—and arguably the most important— transition that took place at Cahokia in the early days of its inception concerned climate. The atmosphere of the American continent just prior to the time of Cahokia's "big bang" can best be characterized as undergoing a period of intensive warming. This gradual heating, which ultimately signaled the impending collapse of Cahokia's Mayan neighbors to the south, inevitably spelled drought for many Mesoamericans. For Native Americans residing in and around the Mississippi Valley on the cusp of the Late Woodland and Early Mississippian phases, however, this thermal escalation meant an immoderate multiplication of moisture on the mainland. Between the swelling of the rivers and the overall increase in precipitation, this progressive warming quickly transformed the arid prairies of the Midwest into the vast floodplains known as the American Bottom. It wasn't simply rainfall, moreover, but a more predictable rainfall, the cycles of which were both foreseeable and dependable—that is, until they weren't.

It is conceivably difficult for many readers to grasp the magnitude of this transition—which is understandable. Luckily, water is a natural resource that the majority of modern Western humans are possessed of the luxury of simply taking for granted. For example, except for certain isolated instances, rather than be faced with the question of sufficient supplies of water, we in the West tend to worry instead primarily about which *brand* we want to buy. Sans the marketing and the capitalistic setting, the situation at Cahokia became something similar. Water was not a resource of which Cahokians were in want. Ergo, for the many cases of those who had experienced the reality of thirst, dehydration, and drought, wheresoever dispersed, Cahokia quickly developed into a safe haven and destination city. For, surely, the powers that be were smiling upon the city of Cahokia.

CAHOKIA'S CORN

The Early Mississippians lived an essentially hunter-gatherer lifestyle that was compact and nomadic. But along with the increase of water in Cahokia came a number of new Native settlers, contributing to a rise in the potential for the emergence of a revolutionary, unprecedented art: agriculture.[8] And, as it just so happens, right around the time that Cahokian water supplies initially started to surge, maize—that is, corn, a crop that would reshape the face of the Eastern Woodlands— first began to appear in the Mississippi Valley. Before it arrived in the Southeast in 1000 CE, maize had been grown in the Southwest for roughly three thousand years—and in Mesoamerica for some six thousand before that. As it turned out, the novel marshy conditions developing around Cahokia proved ideal for the production and surplus of maize—which is fortuitous insofar as it would take in the vicinity of a million ears per year to sustain Cahokia's expanding population. That's a lot of grain. To maintain that degree of cereal output, clearly, a supernatural's assistance would be necessitated—and that is precisely the role in which a nonhuman person, known as the Maize or Earth Mother, was envisaged. She was also sometimes referred to as Evening Star. Several flint clay statues depicting this goddess, that were later fashioned into ceremonial pipes, have been recovered from Cahokia and related regions. In Desha County, Arkansas, for example, a beautiful Cahokian artifact known as the Westbrook figurine—previously cataloged as the McGehee figure pipe—was found. Were there any question as to the cereal and vegetable nature of this particular preternatural person, the artisan(s) responsible for fashioning the piece took considerable care to depict delicate, detailed cornstalks and sunflowers as surreally sprouting straight from her palms. It's a stunning piece. Behind the kneeling figure is shown a sacred bundle (i.e., a portable container of cult paraphernalia) in the form of a *petaca* or woven basket, from which this generous grain goddess looks to emerge. In fact, it was probably as just such a sacred, bundled petaca that maize and its flint clay goddess were first delivered unto the Amerindians of the Southeast. Oftentimes, such bundles originated from personal dreams or vision quests, with the associated spirit generally instructing the dreamer in the particular petaca's proper mode of preparation. Through its totemic materialization, one such vision could potentially sustain several generations throughout the centuries—the initial inspiration acquiring an almost archetypal weight, expanding into a sacred legend that explained the source and function of the petaca.[9] Similar to the Westbrook figurine, the female character shown kneeling upon ears of corn that is embellished upon the Keller figurine—believed to depict the Corn Mother as well—has her right hand resting upon an identical woven basket, a cornstalk in her left. Cornstalks also sprout from effeminate hands on the partially reconstructed Sponemann figurine. Like the comparable Willoughby figurine recovered from the same site, the Sponemann statue was irreparably damaged—but not so much that the deity was unrecognizable. There is little question in regard to the identity of this supernatural. Another female form featuring obvious vegetable traits and discovered near Cahokia is the Birger figurine. Found alongside the Keller figurine at the BBB Motor Site, the Birger figurine is unique in that, instead of manually sprouting cornstalks or sunflowers, the clenched fist of this depiction of the goddess grasps what appears to be a short-handled gardening hoe. Although, rather than disturb the face of the earth, our vegetable venerable instead digs into the back of a fat, curved, split-tailed snake—one that happens to be possessed of a feline head and a decidedly *toothy mouth*.[10] As opposed to a petaca, in this curious case, the grain goddess appears to emerge directly from the coil of the accompanying serpent. Moreover, out of the tail of this beast, at the point where it parts into a pair, protrude fruiting vines filled with gourds—the variety used to prepare ritual rattles—that climb up the back of our gardening goddess. In addition to sunflower seeds, kernels of maize, and the anthropomorphic flint clay pipes, the sacred rattles created from these godly gourds were doubtless an integral part of the ritual paraphernalia bundled within Corn Mother's priestly petaca. Furthermore, the advent of maize agriculture coincided with a drastic uptick in the degree of artistic expression regarding shamanic and trance-related artifacts.[11] We'll learn more about the Maize Mother and her thunderous Hero Twins below.

Notably, in the act of fashioning these already-ancient idols into fully functional pipes, the devotees were in fact forming a direct line of communication with their patron deities. By puffing powerful psychoactive herbs, such as Aztec tobacco (*Nicotiana rustica*), jimsonweed (*Datura stramonium*), black nightshade, and *kinni-kinnick* (which will be addressed below), through the ceremonial conduit opened up via the very representation on the pipe itself, worshippers could effectively invoke the physical presence of their gods and goddesses, making supplications and receiving their blessings in a very visceral way. Moreover, the ritual action of smoking from the pipe in effect *animated* the effigy— that is, it *ensouled* the figurine—veritably calling down the presence of the preternatural person presented in the piece.

> The reason so many flint clay statuettes were created as pipes or redrilled as pipes shortly after completion was that tobacco as a primary ritual substance possessed the ability to animate the flint clay statuettes. Thus, burning the potent sense-altering vegetal matter, transmuting it into smoke, activated the actual supernatural ritual participants, rather than simply serving as artistic metaphors for making ritual contact with the corresponding spirit.[12]

This angle becomes increasingly apparent in the divine diorama of pipes positioned in the tableau organized in the Spirit Lodge of Craig Mound at Spiro.

CAHOKIA'S CORRESPONDENCE

We have seen how Cahokia, in its design, accurately referenced the tripartite cosmos. Even in the Middle World, though, Cahokians were able to accurately embody and harness the powers present in the skies. Truly, insofar as it faithfully reflected astronomical phenomena in its terrestrial layout, Cahokia could quite literally be called heaven on earth. To illustrate, in the humid flood-plains of the American Bottom, located about twenty-three kilometers east of Cahokia, stands a unique hilltop ridge that is perched atop a seeping water table. This remarkable feature is part of a significant ceremonial site, known by archaeologists as the Emerald Acropolis, which aligns naturally and perfectly with a rare astral occurrence called a maximum northern moonrise—an octakaidecadal (every 18.6 years, to be exact) astrological event known as a lunistice or lunar standstill.[13] Lunistices form the lunar counterpart to the more recognizable annual phenomena of solar standstills—better known as solstices. Conceivably, both solar and lunar standstills played significant roles in the rituals, mythologies, and cosmologies of the Mississippian peoples. However, it was with reference to the natural orientation of the Emerald Acropolis— and therefore specifically to the moon itself—that the early Cahokians took to aligning their city. Other sites are aligned this way. A little over four kilometers from this Emerald Acropolis stands another anomalous site that archaeologists associate with Cahokia. At the Pfeffer site, rectangular ritual structures were raised, razed, and rebuilt again and again, repeatedly realigning these little houses with *something* locatable on the horizon. We now know that *something* to have been the moon—the minimum and maximum northern moonrises, to be exact. In point of fact, one particular structure at the Pfeffer site has managed to retain both these correspondences. The hut itself is oriented to the minimum northern moonrise, while a diagonal, oblong, oval-shaped trench, stretching from one corner to the other, cuts its way across the mixed clay floor. This enigmatic addition was found to align precisely with the maximum northern moonrise.[14] However, the function of this furrow is not well understood. Perhaps they simply grew tired of rebuilding.

One more district worth mentioning in this regard lies a whopping six hundred kilometers from the precinct of Cahokia. In what is now Trempealeau County in west-central Wisconsin, every 18.6 years—that is, on the anniversary of the minimum northern moonrise—Cahokians would go through the terrific trouble of traveling against the grain of the river, canoeing up the Mississippi, to arrive at an isolated ceremonial site known as Trempealeau. There we find an extraordinary ridge, to which the rest of the site is oriented, that perfectly and *unnaturally* aligns with the minimum northern moonrise. I say it is unnatural because, by extensively cutting and filling the landscape, Cahokians spent considerable hours terraforming the bluff of the ridge, reorienting it precisely to the northern minimum lunistice.[15] If the other sites weren't completely convincing of a Cahokian predilection for all things lunar, surely the extreme effort exhibited at Trempealeau is enough to persuade.

A potential explanation for this marked preoccupation with the moon may in fact be partly aeromantic. For Cahokia to maintain its momentum, adequate rainfall was absolutely essential. Before the advent of modern meteorology, the prediction of future weather conditions was predicated almost entirely upon reading into the configurations of the skies. A good example is the well-known adage—alluded to even in the gospel of St. Matthew—that says, *Red sky at night, shepherd's* (or *sailor's*) *delight; red sky in the morning, shepherd's warning.* Scarlet skies at dusk indicate moderate atmospheric conditions for the following day, while a ruby-colored sky observed early at dawn is a sure sign of considerable rain to come. For the ancient Cahokians, instead of sunrises or sunsets, the moon—specifically, paraselenae—appears to have fulfilled that predictive role. A paraselene—the lunar version of the more well-known parhelion or sun dog and known sometimes as a moon dog (not to be confused with the person known as the Viking of Sixth Avenue)—is a prism-like atmospheric optical phenomenon, observable precisely twenty-two degrees to the left or right of the quarter to full moon. Caused by the refraction of moonlight by hexagonal-plate-shaped ice crystals contained in cirrus and cirrostratus cloud formations,[16] the appearance of a paraselene on both sides of the satellite is a clear indication that rain is sure to fall within the next twenty-four to seventy-two hours. Significantly, it has been argued that this tripartite design—namely, three linear points, the central node being larger than the two flanking it—fed into the arrangements of certain important Cahokian sites. The trio of mounds constructed atop the artificially oriented ridge situated in Trempealeau, Wisconsin, for instance, are organized according to that very same plan.[17]

CAHOKIA'S CATHARSIS

Around the same time that Cahokia was coalescing in what is now East St. Louis, the landscape of the American Bottom also witnessed the emergence of a new religious movement(s) among its Indigenous inhabitants, the evidence for which is a number of curious circular platform mounds—as opposed to heap-style or angular mounds—that began showing up roughly a century before the turn of the first millennium. In many cases, these miniature mesas were made to align with one of the four aforementioned lunistices. At the Emerald Acropolis, for example, positioned perpendicular to Mound 12—a seven-meter-high, two-tiered platform mound and the centerpiece of the site—are a series of circular platform mounds that align perfectly with the maximum northern moonrise.[18] One of these is even found atop Mound 12, situated on the northwest corner. In fact, that is true also of Monk's Mound at Cahokia, where not only was it plotted in the same place on the mound as at Emerald (i.e., the northwest corner), but it is this feature—and not the central point of the mound itself—with which the Rattlesnake Causeway was made to align.[19] These structures were therefore important indeed.

Erected specifically with the annular shape of the full moon in mind,[20] placed in close proximity to what have been called shrine houses, Cahokia's circular platform mounds are believed by archaeologists to have been the elevated foundations for sudatoria—sweat lodges—which made their North American debut with the advent of the Mississippians. A sudatorium is a small, man-made, dome-shaped, cave-like structure, framed with eight small poles and saplings and covered in alternating layers of birch bark, blankets, and animal skins. Usually in the center of the structure was dug a hearth—a small depression in the floor, similar to a sipapu (p. 31) in the Southwest—where heated stones were placed and over which water was repeatedly poured for the purpose of producing formidable steam. Serving a sympathetic magical function, this steam was likely envisaged by bathers as a ritual reproduction of the atmospheric conditions necessary for producing paraselenes—and thus rain. Moreover, the Mississippians were well aware of the purgative properties of "sweating." Much like their use of emetics before going into battle or prior to undergoing a sacred rite, Indigenous Americans would resort to a small stint in the sudatorium in advance of almost any important undertaking. In the Midéwiwin, for instance, which consisted of four (or sometimes eight) degrees into which one had to be initiated, a candidate was expected to retire to the sudatorium prior to participating in every single grade of advancement.

Furthermore, the Ojibwa or Chippewa of the Great Lakes region had a special group of mystics, known as Bear visionaries, which included all tribesmen who had dreamed of Bear—a powerful Manitou supernatural said to have delivered, in the form of several sacred bundles, the "religious" rites of the Midéwiwin unto the Anishinaabe. In addition to ritually abstaining from the consumption of bear meat (save during certain ceremonies, where participation was considered compulsory), Bear visionaries were united in their collective involvement in a "terrible" sweating ordeal, known as a Bear lodge. This designation is not surprising as the sudatorium itself somewhat resembled a makeshift bear's den. The protocols for ordinary sweat lodges called for the heating and cooling of sixteen stones. A Bear lodge, on the other hand, employed no less than eighty stones, which were continually reheated for hours on end—the visionaries inside gradually assuming the form and characteristics of their Manitou patron. Covered perhaps in sacred bearskins, the lodge itself was envisaged as the cavernous insides of an enormous bear.[21] This was also true of a "common" sudatorium, as Landes's informant, Pindigegizig, explained:

"for our Grandfather [Bear] told the Indian to get in under him and then he dropped his hide over him." Similarly, even the sweat lodge stakes or framework were formally saluted as "Bear's legs."[22]

The recent discovery of the aforementioned circular platform mounds, and of the sweat lodges evidenced to have been erected atop them, has forced archaeologists to reconsider their theories in regard to the stimulus that could have attracted so many to Cahokia. It is now becoming clear that one of the chief appeals that drew people to the city was likely the curative and analeptic virtues associated with these very same sacred sudatoria.[23]

CAHOKIA'S COURTS

Another key factor that lured pilgrims to the city of Cahokia was a recreational game or sport, called chunkey. I say recreational, but really it was nothing of the sort. Here in the modern West, we prefer our lifeways to be strictly demarcated. For instance, we tend to view religion, recreation, politics, and so on as separate domains of human activity—divided into their own neat, manageable boxes. The Establishment Clause of the United States Bill of Rights is a perfect example. However, these thick lines in the sand were not drawn by Amerindians, who understood all things not only to be interconnected, but to be incorporated in—and interspersed with—the sacred. And chunkey was certainly no exception. Indeed, one might even go so far as to say that the game was among the most sanctified pastimes in all of Cahokia. For we will find that chunkey was possessed of profound mythological and cosmological significance.

Unlike the Mayan pastime *pok-ta-pok*, chunkey was not a ballgame, although the two did have a lot in common, right down to their origin stories or "charters." Where pok-ta-pok was played with a heavy rubber ball (or even stones), chunkey was instead carried out by two opposing teams using spear-like rivercane sticks. These wooden poles were expertly hurled in the direction of a rolling, wheel-like, semi-smooth stone, known as a discoidal—or simply called a chunkey stone. The charter for this ritual game was a legend concerning a pair of powerful thunder

⊙ ⊙ ⊙

Fig. 3.2. The Hero Twins as depicted on the wall of Picture Cave. See also color plate 7.
Photo by the author

and lightning supernaturals, called the Hero Twins, known under the names Lodge-Boy and Thrown-Away (among other titles, depending on the region). Myths concerning the adventures of the Hero Twins appear to be nearly universal among American Natives—from Canada all the way down to South America. American anthropologist, Paul Radin, for instance, characterized the Hero Twins narratives as the "basic North

American myth."[24] Its basic formula consists of the decapitation of the Twins' father—likely identical with Red Horn—and the subsequent burial of the cranium below the chunkey court. After defeating the powers of darkness in a cosmic game of chunkey, the Twins recover and restore the head of the father—his body resurrected by the boy known as Thrown-Away, who possesses the power of reanimation. We will return to the myth of the Hero Twins in chapter seven.

Disturbingly, archaeological evidence suggests that there may have been more at stake for these players than simple bragging rights and vainglory. It has been proposed that the deadly serious game of chunkey could have resulted in the very real decapitation of members of losing teams, thereby commemorating the mythical decapitation and (temporary) destruction of the Twins' father. Supporting evidence for this proposal includes a number of depictions of cheering chunkey "warriors," including images of the so-called Birdman—a mace-wielding avi-anthropomorphic, shaman-like figure preserved on marine shell medicine cups and in copper repoussé plates—brandishing the severed heads of what some have identified as losing team members. According to this hypothesis, the heads are probably not those of the opposing teams, as both the celebrating player and the head he's shown flaunting in many cases share the same facial decorations—a common device used to express identity and solidarity.[25] And, indeed, no less than four headless skeletons were recovered from the infamous Mound 72 at Cahokia—a burial mound located next to the Rattlesnake Causeway, between the Rattlesnake and Monk Mounds. However, as we will see in chapter seven (note 14 on p. 115), following an important discovery by a team of talented researchers, these heads that the chunkey players carry may not be flesh and blood human craniums at all, but rather human head effigy pots, a number of which have been found throughout the Southeast. Significantly, Mound 72 also featured the lavish Birdman burial. The Birdman burial is unique in that it held the remains of a man perfectly positioned upon a raptor-like cape, sewn directly into his skin, of shell beads designed to resemble a falcon or eagle with outstretched wings. Initially, this lavish burial was thought to be for a village chief

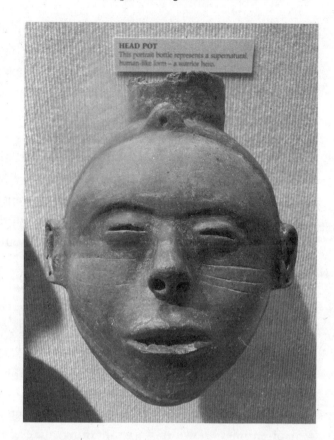

HEAD POT
This portrait bottle represents a supernatural, human-like form – a warrior hero.

⊚ ⊚ ⊚
Fig. 3.3. Human head effigy pot.
Photo by the author

or perhaps even a shaman. However, the discovery of a second skeleton buried back-to-back with the first, face down and immediately beneath the raptor-shell cape, has made it apparent that these flying figures most likely signify our two Hero Twins in their Thunderbird aspects.

Chunkey was also likely possessed of an esoteric yet practical significance, specifically related to the survival of the soul after the death of the body. Recall that, in the case of the Path of Souls, the spirit of the deceased had to be launched at the ogee in the Hand constellation in the form of an arrow. This is a fairly common motif in the Southeastern Ceremonial Complex. "Through magical arrows stored in sacred bundles," archaeologist David H. Dye tell us, for instance, "the Twins could escape from or discomfit an antagonist by transforming themselves into arrows that could be shot over long distances."[26] Moreover, Lankford writes that the myths of various Native peoples "speak of heroic figures who are able to fly through the air or up to the sky by transforming themselves into [. . .] arrows."[27] In another example, the supernatural figure of Red Horn is able to defeat the warrior spirit, Turtle, in a foot race, "after repeatedly projecting himself forward as an arrow."[28] In the game of chunkey, it is likely that the chunkey stick signifies the soul in flight, while the discoidal relates to the ogee portal, which is comparable to a moving target insofar as the threshold effectively disappears below the line of the horizon shortly after its point of opening—that is, just before sunrise in and around the winter solstice. In this regard, the chunkey courts were quite literally training grounds for the Path of Souls journey.

Chunkey was a central part of Cahokian life. This was true not only for the players, but also for those who came to the city from far and wide simply to observe—and to place dire bets on—those involved in the games. Not unlike modern-day sporting events, gambling was just another integral part of the chunkey experience. And the consequences were oftentimes just as destructive. At the prospect of vicariously winning through the victorious team members, chunkey gamblers were oftentimes known to wager anything and everything in their possession, including their own freedom and families. So invested were these gamblers in the athletes and outcomes, suicide is said to have been completely commonplace among those unfortunate enough to have caught a losing streak.[29]

CAHOKIA'S CASSINA

Where the Natives of Chaco Canyon—Cahokia's Southwestern "Lunar Twin"[30]—had distinctive cylinder jars for the ceremonial consumption of their caffeine-rich, Central American cacao (as evidenced by the cache discovered in Room 28 of Pueblo Bonito), Cahokians received their caffeine fix from equally characteristic beaker-style vessels and shell cups. From these, Cahokians consumed copious amounts of another caffeinated ritual concoction, called by the Timucua *cassina*—better

⊚ ⊚ ⊚
Fig. 3.4. The caffeine-rich
Ilex vomitoria served as
the base for various "black
drink" ceremonial blends.
Photo by the author

known as black drink.[31] Closely related to South America's yerba-maté (*Ilex paraguariensis*)—although considerably more potent—cassina is the only source of caffeine native to North America. However, it is not known to grow near Cahokia. Instead, indicating its importance to the Indigenous there, city officials had incredible amounts of the plant imported from the regions where it did flourish—areas such as Mississippi, Alabama, Georgia, and Florida. Prepared from the serrated leaves of the southeastern evergreen shrub, yaupon holly (*Ilex vomitoria*), cassina had to be thoroughly dried and toasted before being boiled, strained, and reduced to a "black drink." Toasting or roasting the leaves was an essential part of the rite. This rendered the considerable concentrations of caffeine contained in the shrub more bioavailable, thus "activating" the brew. Intimately intertwined, both black drink and the use of shell drinking cups were clearly possessed of profound religious significance for Cahokians, closely associated with ceremonial life in the American Bottom. Notably, judging by the prevalence of shell cups interred as burial goods in Hopewellian and preceding cultures, the use of black drink may stretch back even into the Archaic Period.[32]

Amerindians of the Southeast indulged in cassina for three reasons: (1) as a beverage whose function was to stimulate social cohesion, much like the role of tea and coffee today; (2) as a "medicine broth," both for physiological and psychological healing; and (3) *sometimes* as an emetic.[33] When cassina consumption was first observed by the encroaching French and Spanish, it was noted that the ritual was limited to the men of the tribes only—namely, the nobility and the warrior class—who were in the habit of convening at least every other day (if not more often) to imbibe the inky *Ilex* from enormous, intricately carved emperor helmet (*Cassis madagascariensis*), horse conch (*Triplofusus giganteus* or *Pleuroploca gigantea*), and especially lightning whelk (*Busycon contrarium*) shell cups.[34] A number of extraordinary engravings by Jacques Le Moyne, the first French artist to visit the American continent, neatly show their use in funerary, wartime, and political ritual contexts, although the report of eighteenth-century botanist Mark Catesby, as well as the discovery of these same shell cups buried in graves alongside adolescents, females, and even small children,[35] has called into question this reported masculocentric limitation of the ritual. Imported all the way from the Gulf Coast, *Busycon contrarium* was clearly the preferred shell for ceremonial cassina consumption in Cahokia. They were prized over other varieties for the simple reason that they are "left-handed"—that is, the broad end of lightning whelk shells spirals widdershins, unlike emperor helmet and horse conch shells, which exclusively turn deasil. We learned earlier that it was none other than Makwa Manito, the Bear supernatural of the Midé, who brought the sacred bundles of the Midéwiwin to the Grand Medicine Society. Those wishing to honor the Bear supernatural, such as the Bear Clan of the Hocąk or Winnebago people, for instance, did so by feasting on Bear's favorite foods—e.g., honey, maple sugar, and sweet berries—*using only their left hands*. The reader may be asking, "What has sinistral dexterity to do with bears?"—to which I reply with the following anecdote from a story regarding Shaggy Man:

> Shaggy Man shot a great thicket of arrows at the bears standing about, and many were felled. The inhabitants of the bear village scattered in every direction. There was an orphan bear who lived at the edge of the village. As he hurriedly tried to put his moccasins on, he put them on the wrong feet. So ever after the feet of bears have been turned out the wrong way.[36]

This legendary tale explains why bear tracks, as opposed to the tracks of humans, turn outward, as though they have their "moccasins" placed on the wrong feet. The right arm of Bear, therefore, is thought to culminate in a left hand. In fact, this is why the Kutenai name for Makwa Manito translates to "Left-Handed One."[37] Similarly, a flint clay effigy pipe originating in Cahokia, known as Grizzlyman on account of the bear claws worn in the figure's earlobes, clasps in his left hand a severed deer cranium as an indication of his namesake. In the Osage language, the title of this Lord of the Pleiades translates to "He-Who-Holds-a-Deer-Head-in-His-Left-Hand."[38] The close association of cassina ceremonies with left-handed paraphernalia may go far in explaining the recovery of *Ilex* seeds alongside the bones of one or more black bears (*Ursus americanus*) from a public structure—possibly a temple—at the Cherokee site of Coweeta Creek in North Carolina.[39]

Apropos the third application enumerated above, the observation that Natives tended to drink, vomit, and drink the beverage again and again in a single session has led some commentators to suspect that yaupon holly was an effective emetic—a powerful purgative potation used for the purpose of purifying the people, both in body and in soul—hence the botanical classification, *vomitoria*. And, cassina was indeed employed in this way. In fact, so prevalent was the association of yaupon with purity and catharsis, despite its dark coloration, that some tribes referred to *Ilex* instead as "white drink."[40] However, as we noted above, even in excessive doses *Ilex vomitoria* alone does not seem to induce vomiting. As it turns out, on top of the common cassina ceremony, where the holly tea was consumed by itself, without any added ingredients, yaupon was also regularly used as a basic carrier for a number of other sacred and medicinal plants. These unusual additions appear to fall into at least two separate categories: (1) emetic and (2) entheogenic.

In the case of the former, herbs regularly added to cassina include: button snakeroot, also known as rattlesnake master (*Eryngium aquaticum*), northern blue flag iris (*Iris versicolor*), red willow bark (*Salix laevigata*)—called *cansasa* by some Native cultures—and finally Indian tobacco or puke weed (*Lobelia inflata*).[41] Snakeroot, for instance, was used early on as a war medicine, both to purge prior to, and protect the warrior during, raids and battles. The name arises from its ancient use as a treatment for snakebite. Notably, enslaved African Americans also prized rattlesnake master, often adding the roots of this powerful plant to their *paquet congo*–like gris-gris bags—a magical pouch, similar to a midéwayan—for the purpose of speeding up a given conjuration. Another emetic, northern blue flag, was employed by some Native Americans also as an antiseptic, an antiparasitic, and an analgesic. The steamed roots of this special species of iris were even believed to have been helpful in protecting its users both from physical and from magical attacks. Red willow bark is an essential ingredient in a number of sacred *kinni-kinnick* smoking blends. Possessed of salicin and salicylic acid, Mother Nature's answer to over-the-counter aspirin, willow barks have a long history of use as anti-inflammatories and analgesics. In standard doses, the plant is perfectly safe and even beneficial to ingest. However, in the concentrations in which Natives seem to have been brewing various forms of cassina (i.e., into a black syrup), salicylate overdose—which would certainly induce vomiting, in addition to a number of other unpleasant side effects—cannot be ruled out from our list of emetic culprits. The last additive, *Lobelia inflata*, is known as puke weed and Indian tobacco, making it a strong candidate for cassina's cathartic action. Indeed, much like button snakeroot, this annual or biennial herbaceous plant has a long history of use as a powerful purgative. This is true especially among Cherokee Natives, who used the herb even to quell tobacco cravings. Complicating matters, though, both *Salix laevigata* and *Lobelia inflata* have their own adumbrated inebriating effects. According to one 1848 report,

> [red willow bark] has a highly narcotic effect on those not habitu-
> ated to its use, and produces a heaviness sometimes approaching stu-
> pefaction, altogether different from the soothing effects of tobacco.[42]

Likewise, lobelia contains lobeline—a psychoactive alkaloid that has been qualified as a hallucinogen. Ergo, *Salix laevigata* and *Lobelia inflata* may straddle each of our aforementioned categories of additive, both emetic and entheogenic. It is also possible that secretive substances of an unknown nature were added to black drink. We'll return to this possibility below.

Notably, red willow bark and lobelia—along with *Nicotiana* sp., bearberry (*Arctostaphylos uva-ursi*), bear root or oshá (*Ligusticum porteri*), and a slew of other herbs—are also common supplements in various forms of kinni-kinnick—sacred smoking blends revered by a number of Indigenous North American peoples, including Algonquin, Lakota or Dakota, Menominee, Odaawaa, Ojibwe or Chippewa, Shoshoni, and Winnebago-speaking tribes.[43] Kinni-kinnick is probably bearberry, which was "the main alternative smoke plant to tobacco in many parts of the Pacific Northwest Coast," both with and without tobacco. However, as one pair of researchers has noted,

> kinni-kinnick is a general term that can also refer to other plants
> smoked in this region, including Yew (*Taxus brevifolia*) needles,
> Dogwood (*Cornus* sp.) leaves, Salal (*Gaultheria shallon*) leaves, and
> Madrone (*Arbutus menziesii*) leaves.[44]

Regarding other possible entheogenic additives incorporated into special black drink blends, secondary plant remains discovered in the analyses of various botanical assemblages recovered from important Mississippian sites where shell cups were also found include: Aztec tobacco (*Nicotiana rustica*), black nightshade (*Solanum ptycanthum*), jimsonweed (*Datura stramonium*), and morning glory seeds, each of which will be addressed in chapter seven.

All of these novel factors (and more) surely contributed to the enigmatic emergence of Cahokia as a booming, popular destination city. But while the MIIS persisted right up until the time of the arrival of the Spanish, the same cannot be said of Cahokia itself. For reasons not fully understood, although likely involving devastating drought conditions—brought on by the Little Ice Age—that obliterated the city's production of maize, residents of Cahokia abandoned the American Bottom and spread to other, more dependable areas of Southeastern North America.[45] One of those areas was Spiro, Oklahoma. In the middle of the fourteenth century CE, around the same time that Cahokia was experiencing its sudden and rapid decline, this Caddoan Mississippian mound complex, over seven hundred kilometers southwest of Cahokia, emerged to fill the gaping wound left by the dissolution of North America's first large-scale city.

lore of the Spiro community. Even during the time of the University of Oklahoma's excavations at the site, it is said that none of the descendants would dare even approach the site—especially after sundown.[1]

When the trove sleeping in Craig Mound finally was disturbed, it was roused by a group of decidedly despicable men—tomb looters and treasure hunters who were concerned with nothing more than the money to be made by selling the priceless artifacts—calling themselves the Pocola Mining Company (PCM). While Aunt Rachel Brown's apprehensive reticence served to preserve the great mound's ancient integrity, it was a man named George Evans, the warden of Brown's juvenile descendants—the "Craig children"—who, on November 27, 1935, had no problem leasing out Spiro's sacred space to the PCM grave robbers for them to exercise their destructive and exploitative tendencies. From exquisite copper repoussé plates to expertly engraved marine shell cups and impressive flint clay statuettes, what the men uncovered there was formidable and unprecedented. For instance, the thousands of marine shell cups alone numbered at least one hundred times that of all the other Mississippian sites known to archaeologists combined.[2] The acquisition of precious metals and valuable stones being their exclusive drive, the men behind the PCM indiscriminately disposed of many of these objects, as well as their associated human remains, trampling pottery, pipes, and petacas in the irresponsible, impetuous process. Even so, thousands upon thousands of intact relics were taken from the site, billed as "A 'King Tut' Tomb in the Arkansas Valley" in 1935 by *The Kansas City Star*. Those that were not destroyed were quickly distributed, sold to the highest bidders, making their way throughout the continent and across the oceans into both private and public Native American collections.

When biological anthropologist Forrest E. Clements got wind of the tragedy that was befalling Spiro, he attempted to buy the PCM out of their lease—but their greed was insatiable, and the men, with their pickaxes and shovels, continued to hack away at what remained of the central Spiro mound. Clements, distraught, was forced to lobby the state of Oklahoma, who quickly passed legislation preventing the pillaging and pilfering then taking place at the Spiro site—but not before the PCM unearthed a mysterious hollow chamber concealed within the heart of Craig Mound. When the men finally were forced to leave the site, the cist was thoughtlessly stuffed with powerful explosives, and the entrance, along with the majority of the chamber's irreplaceable contents, was totally obliterated. It is only through sketches and notes from the era regarding the objects and organization of the orifice that archaeologists were able to reconstruct and reimagine the revealing makeup of what is now known colloquially as the Spiro Spirit Lodge and Great Mortuary.[3]

The Spirit Lodge was deliberately constructed atop a mass burial from a preceding era. Similar to Monk's Mound's central role at Cahokia, Craig Mound was intended to represent the Mississippian cosmos in miniature, with three distinct layers answering to the Below, Middle, and Sky Worlds envisaged by the SECC. In erecting this subterranean structure, a space was cleared in the center of the Great Mortuary by disinterring the preexisting remains—perhaps Hopewellian—and relocating them to the outer edges of the manmade hillock. This created a circular berm that flanked the Spirit Lodge on all sides, signifying the Below World or realm of the dead. Not unlike other Caddo constructions, such as at Cahokia, in order to effect the creation of an *imago mundi*, effectively finding the "center of the universe," an axis mundi was first placed in the center of the mound. This bridge between the realms being established, the "world tree" was subsequently removed and the building of this new sacred space resumed. For the establishment of the Middle World atop that of the Below, the newly made circular berm was filled in with midden or litter burials—discarded shell cups and ceramic pottery, all broken—to signify the realm wherein living men have their being. Representative of the Path of Souls or Milky Walkway, the surface of the layer of litter was covered with a wooden veneer of carefully installed split-cane flooring, with the orientation of the planks being just off a north-south axis. This, once more, is characteristic of Caddo constructions such as those at Cahokia, indicating a preoccupation with each of the lunistices and with the Milky Way—

that is, with the Path of Souls. It was upon this celestial split-cane base that the Spirit Lodge proper was built—a material manifestation of the Sky World and the supernaturals who were envisaged as existing there. A number of enormous cedar posts—used by the PCM for firewood during their desecration of the site—locked the cavern in place, maintaining an airtight space that effectively preserved the artifacts it contained from being lost to the rich soil that surrounded the cist. This liminal locale, like the idol-housing temples that once stood at the apex of mounds at other Mississippian sites, ritually assumed the place of the Sky World and its inhabitants, constituting the so-called Spirit Lodge proper.

Symbolically arranged about this sacred space, in the precise places where such supernaturals were supposed to reside in the skies— identified with certain significant stellar configurations—was a tableau or diorama of Mississippian nonhuman entities in the form of sizable wooden idols and drilled pipe statuettes. As we saw with the orientation of the split-cane flooring, these cult statues were interred on a north-south axis, with a Birdman effigy pipe, known as Big Boy, and a rattlesnake-stemmed elbow pipe, probably representing the Great Serpent (Scorpius), positioned along the centerline in the extreme north. The ears of this Birdman effigy are adorned with long-nosed maskettes—representative of the Hero Twins—typical of the cultural hero, Red Horn, who is also known by the name He-Who-Wears-Human-Heads-in-His-Ears. He is also identified as Morning Star. Immediately behind this combination of images was placed a set of seven chipped and polished ceremonial stone maces—a bit of ritual regalia specifically associated with Birdman iconography. In the center of this Sky World replica were found two additional drilled pipe statuettes. One of these was prepared in imitation of the Corn or Earth Mother, sometimes known as Evening Star, the consort of the aforementioned Morning Star deity. Placed directly to her right is another pipe—a "raptor-over-recumbent-human"—no doubt serving as a mode of evocation for the supernatural figure, the Raptor on the Path (Cygnus), whose final judgment determines the ultimate fate of one's soul. It should be evident at this point that these pipe-idols indicated obstacles encountered by the soul in the course of traversing the Path of Souls and would have been filled with smokable "medicines" designed or intended either to invoke the presence of the supernatural fashioned into the pipe or as an apotropaic to protect the soul from confrontation with that very same nonhuman entity. Deliberately positioned in pairs, these four pipes present to their viewer first the "giver of human life" (Birdman) and "the taker" (Great Serpent), and second, the "source-of-fertility" (Corn Mother) and the spirit representing "death and transformation."[4] Finally, in the extreme south, there lay three large wooden human effigies—statues, not pipes—suggestive no doubt of the First Man and his immediate descendants. These effigies marked the southern entry point for shamans and for the deceased that leads one onto the celestial Milky Walkway. To the east and west of this north-south centerline, creating the likeness of a Tau-style cross, were placed woven petacas housing the regalia of the gods, *Olivella dama* shell beads from the Gulf of California, repoussé plates, and as many as thirty ceremonial axes—the latter two bundled sets being composed completely of copper. Lastly, encircling the whole diorama were innumerable enormous lightning whelk shell cups, mostly intact, having "unique decoration" executed primarily in the Craig and Braden styles. The result is something reminiscent of an Amerindian type of Mithraeum.[5] Truly, given the large number of carved shell cups and deific effigy pipes deposited in the space, it is not inconceivable that this liminal locale served as a sort of Native American answer to certain of the chambers of the initiation employed by some Greco-Roman mystery cults—a "Mississippian *telesterion*," to borrow a term from Eleusis—where, instead of drinking *kykeon* from a ceremonial *krater*,[6] various cassina blends, including *Datura* spp., black nightshade, morning glory spp., and potentially *Missihuasca*, were imbibed from intricately carved marine shell cups and incised pottery for the purpose of calling forth the supernatural shown upon the vessel. Moreover, in awakening the potency resident within the effigy pipes, sacred smokes such as *Datura* spp., *N. rustica*, and black nightshade further assisted the affiliated aspirants in affecting the ascent and eventual divinization of their own souls, as the same progressed nominally and virtually upon the Milky Way Path. In a revealing lecture delivered at the James A. Little Theater in Santa Fe, New Mexico, to the Society for Advanced Research in 2019, F. Kent Reilly III perceptively compared this Mississippian vignette to the Roman Catholic tradition of the "Stations of the Cross."[7]

After successfully reconstructing the contents of the Spirit Lodge hidden inside of Craig Mound at Spiro, it was found that the arrangement of the diorama faithfully adhered to a model of the heavens as the same as was depicted on a three-hundred-year-old buckskin artifact, known as the Skidi Pawnee star chart, currently housed at the Field Museum of Natural History in Chicago, Illinois. Like the Spirit Lodge, the star chart reflects the Milky Way Path of Souls and, in the form of constellations imagined as petacas, the various stations of the supernaturals envisaged as existing there. Discovered in the "Big Black Meteoric Star Bundle"—a Skidi Pawnee petaca—analysis conducted in 1983 at Bell Laboratories in Murray Hill, New Jersey, revealed that this buckskin star chart correctly recorded the exact positions of the heavens on the early morning of February 19, 634 CE—a date onto which some Indigenous North Americans projected the precise timing of the dawn of creation. To be sure, the Spirit Lodge does in fact resemble to a great degree the well-ordered structure of Pawnee earth lodges, of which Spiro's Spirit Lodge may in fact be a special type of variant. This close correlation with the Skidi Pawnee star chart has led some researchers to suggest that the specific function of the Spirit Lodge at Spiro was an attempt to magically "restart time"—returning the Mississippian peoples to what Romanian religious historian Mircea Eliade referred to as *in illo tempore*—the temporal answer to the role of the axis mundi in regard to creating sacred space. The Spirit Lodge may therefore have been nothing short of a large-scale ritual project directed toward correcting the devastating drought conditions caused by the onset of the Little Ice Age—beginning in and around the turn of the fourteenth century—thereby remitting and resetting all of creation back to a perhaps paradisiacal zero point, to borrow a term from the domain of physics.[8]

Spiro remains one of the premier destination spots for those interested and invested in Native American cultures. Even with all of the destruction and looting that took place during the Great Depression, the beauty and grandeur of Spiro still echoes out from the sinusoidal-like ripple that is Craig Mound, not unlike an earthbound beacon, luring its admirers back to this sacred site, year after year, just as it did roughly eight centuries ago. Dare I say, Spiro veritably constitutes the Southeastern equivalent of the *omphalos*—the navel of the world—once housed at Delphi in Phocis, Greece, prior to its destruction by Theodosius I and Arcadius in the fourth century CE, and may rightly be considered the axis mundi of the entire Mississippian Ideological Interaction Sphere.

FIVE

LOST MARBLES AT ETOWAH

In stark contrast to the devastating and irreparable damage wreaked upon the sacred site of Spiro in Oklahoma, there remains in Bartow County, Georgia, another important MIIS "town" that has been hailed as "the most intact Mississippian culture site in the Southeast," known as *Etowah*.[1] I say town because the word *Etowah* is derived from the Muscogee term *italwa*, literally meaning "town." As we'll soon learn, Etowah is home to one of the most significant archaeological discoveries of the entire MIIS. Similar to Spiro, with its Pawnee-like Spirit Lodge, the village of Etowah constitutes a series of earth lodge–style mounds, all centered around a trio of expansive platform mounds, the most impressive of which is Mound A—a platform mound known as Temple Mound—which towers some nineteen meters high and covers at its base no less than three acres. It is the relatively smaller, cone-shaped Mound C, however, currently rising only ten meters high, that will occupy our attention in the present discussion.

Constructed in seven distinct building phases spanning 125 years, Mound C was home to no less than 366 Native American burials before it was excavated, over the course of 77 years, by three separate teams of American archaeologists. The first of these deconstructions, funded by the Bureau of Ethnology, began with a rather shoddy archaeologist named John P. Rogan—after whom the famous Rogan Plates are named—in 1884. Limiting his search to the structure's summit, Rogan reported discovering only eleven burials, all of which contained a number of exquisite copper repoussé plates, carved marine shell gorgets, and various other elaborate grave goods, before moving on to another nearby project. Over four decades later, in 1925, the Robert S. Peabody Foundation funded a second archaeologist, Warren K. Moorehead— known in his day as the Dean of American Archaeology—who added 111 more burial discoveries to Rogan's previous eleven—all located just within the summit of the mound. It wasn't until 1954, however, when the Georgia Historical Commission, believing the mound to be completely exhausted of its secrets and desirous of converting the site into a new state park, enlisted the very able American archaeologist Lewis H. Larson Jr. to clean up Rogan and Moorehead's mess and return the site as closely as possible to its previous condition. It was during Larson's very careful examination of the site, including its base and flanks, that the true significance of Etowah's Mound C really came to light. Over seven years, Larson excavated no fewer than 244 graves from Mound C, literally doubling the number previously found by both Rogan and Moorehead combined.[2]

The vast majority of interments found at Mound C were deposited in the flank surrounding the base of the hill. The remains uncovered by Rogan were found primarily in the summit and center of the structure, contained in elaborate graves lined with cumbersome stone slabs. However, the more significant finds in regard to Mound C's burials were not those contained in the apex and heart of the construction but the individuals interred in Burials 57, 47, and 38, who were concealed in log-lined tombs hidden in the rectangular earthen terrace that extends from the northern quarter of this mortuary mound. Recall that the Path of Souls was specifically associated with the Milky Way's north-south axis, with the southern side constituting the entry point of the Path on the winter solstice and the northern node comprising the final goal for which the soul strove. Those laid to rest in this northern terrace were therefore in all probability individuals who had acquired the highest ranks in the mystical sodality wherein the mysteries of the Path of

Souls were imparted by degrees to select tribesmen via a series of complex and arduous ritual initiations. This hypothesis is supported by the presence of eight lightning whelk shell cups extracted from Burial 57.[3] As we learned in the introduction and in the previous chapter, while these conch cups were employed in the ritual consumption of various hallucinogenic cassina blends, they also served as prestigious badges of attainment, communicating to other members of the tribe their holder's rank and grade within the village's medicine society. Also interred in Burial 57 was a single carved shell gorget, five or six embossed copper repoussé plates, two copper celts, a pair of copper-covered ear spools, one copper bead, and numerous shell beads[4]—likely of the mégis or cowrie variety—the latter of which artfully decorated a collar draped around the neck of the decayed deceased.

As important status symbols similar to the carved conch cups, shell gorgets worn by the Mississippians regularly depicted scenes from Native American mythology and thus arguably showed aspects of the rigorous, religious rituals that were designed to dramatically reflect those very same mythological charters. In the case of the shell gorgets recovered at Etowah, the scenarios, executed in a local style known as Hightower, often evoke lepidopteral imagery associated with an important although relatively obscure moth entity. Known to archaeologists by the pop-cultural epithets Mothra and Mothman, one gorget recovered from Mound C shows a therianthropic, antlered shaman dotted with starlike circles and grasping a giant moth by the proboscis, while he himself sprouts a pair of mothlike wings. His feet, interestingly, are replaced with the sharp claws of an avian raptor. In a similar Hightower-style artifact from Perry County, Missouri— apparently executed by the same craftsman—the shaman grasps two moths, with a proboscis in each hand. His feet, however, are anthropoid and the stellar circles are not present. Another gorget, found at the Hixon site in Tennessee appears to portray the same claw-footed, antlered shaman from Mound C—*twice*. Strangely, the giant moth has disappeared in this case, and instead of grasping the insect's proboscis, he holds a mirror-image of himself by the throat—the

☉ ☉ ☉

Fig. 5.1. Identified as the "tobacco moth," *Manduca sexta,* Mothra or Mothman is a Mississippian supernatural specifically associated with *Datura* and *Nicotiana* spp. See also color plate 3.

Illustration by A. Rivero; Vix Volante Creative

doppelgänger-like twin in turn choking him as well. The symmetrical execution of this particular gorget is breathtakingly skillful, reflective of an obviously highly developed artisanship based at Etowah. A fourth exhibits our antlered, therianthropic shaman, dancing, while brandishing, in the same hand in which he once grasped the moth, a severed head—likely a human head effigy pot—that had been painted to resemble his own. In this instance, his feet are those of a man, while it is his hands that appear raptorial. Still yet a fifth features a similar shapeshifting, antlered shamanic figure, winged and seated cross-legged, who is shown with clawed hands and emerging from what appears to be the bisected chrysalis of a moth or butterfly pupa.[5] The scenes would appear to be somewhat sequential, imparting a powerful model of lepidopteral shamanic transformation. Knight and Franke observe that, iconographically, these gorgets suggest "an intriguing *equivalence* at some level between butterfly [or moth] supernatural and Birdman."[6] I would be inclined to agree. In point of fact, a copper repoussé plate from the Lake Jackson Mounds at Florida shows a typical Birdman motif, brandishing a severed human head, with the long, coiled proboscis of the moth supernatural in place of the standard, curved beak. The Douglas gorget from New Madrid County, Missouri, features the same proboscis—this time on a head-wielding warrior wearing the garb usually associated with Birdman. Curiously, in every case, the Etowah Dances with Mothra gorgets, as the type is known, were interred solely in association with female burials. We'll return to this provocative Mothman supernatural in chapter seven.

For many years, the copper repoussé plates associated with the MIIS were thought to have been donned in a manner identical to that of the shell gorgets—that is, as "symbol badges," "pierced for suspension" and worn in the form of "pendants." But, insofar as the copper plates at Etowah were found under, above, atop, or around the craniums of the decayed individuals with which they were interred, it is clear that these impressive, embossed plates were incorporated into intricate feathered headdresses prepared from hawk skins and held in place by a number of narrow cedar rods.[7] The feathers used in the construction of this headgear were limited to the plumules and downy barbules of birds belonging solely to the *Anatidae* family—that is, ducks, geese, and swans. Consistently described as crowns and like terms in the primary literature, feathered headdresses such as these were documented among the Coosa, the Natchez, the Creeks, and the Timucua. For example, the semianonymous Gentleman of Elvas described the *cacique* (chief) of Coosa as sporting a "diadem of plumes."[8] Similarly, Peruvian chronicler Inca Garcilaso de la Vega relayed that the noblemen who accompanied the cacique of Coosa to his meeting with the Spanish conquistador Hernando de Soto "wore great feather headdresses, these being the adornments of which the natives of this great kingdom are most proud."[9] The eighteenth-century French ethnographer Antoine-Simon Le Page du Pratz explained that the headdress of the Great Sun of the Natchez was a:

> crown [. . .] composed of a cap and a diadem, surmounted by large feathers. The cap is made of a netting, which holds the diadem, which is a texture 2 inches broad and presses together behind tightly as is desired. The cap is of black threads, but the diadem is red and embellished with little beads or small white seeds, as hard as beads. The feathers which surmount the diadem are white. Those in front may be 8 inches long, and those behind 4 inches. These feathers are arranged in a curved line. At the end of these feathers is a tuft of hair [. . .] and above a little hairy tassel [. . .] all being only an inch and a half long and dyed a very beautiful red. This crown or feather hat is an object very pleasing to the sight.[10]

Eighteenth-century American historian James Adair described in detail the "crowns" or headdresses presented to Creek warriors.

> The crown is wrought round with the long feathers of a swan, at the lower end, where it surrounds his temples, and it is curiously weaved with a quantity of white down, to make it sit easy, and appear more beautiful. To this part that wreathes his brows, the skillful artist wraps them close together, a ringlet of the longest feathers of the swan, and turning them carefully upward, in an uniform position, he, in the exact manner, ties them together with deer's sinews, so

that the bandage will not appear to the sharpest eyes without handling it. It is a little open at the top and about fifteen inches high. The crowns they use in constituting leaders, are always worked with feathers of the tail of the cherubic eagle, which causes them to be three or four inches higher than the former.[11]

In response to one of the headdresses pictured by the seventeenth-century French artist Jacques Le Moyne de Morgues, twentieth-century American anthropologist John R. Swanton commented that:

we observe a headband showing a succession of short points as if it were a crown [. . .]. This is all too suggestive of European crowns, and yet in later times, at all events, bands of this pattern, hammered out of silver, were much in use, I myself having seen one that belonged to an Alabama Indian living in Louisiana.[12]

Notably, the presence of feathers in Mississippian art and iconography, known as the petaloid motif, has been identified by Reilly as a type of "celestial symbolic locative," associated specifically with Above World imagery.[13] Even after several centuries, many of these feathers, skillfully dyed in rich red and gold hues, remained intact at Etowah during the time of excavation—especially in Burials 57 and 67, where these "petaloids" were additionally integrated into stunningly detailed checkerboard-patterned robes. Worn atop delicate pearl-embroidered garments, this "feather-faced" ceremonial attire cleverly incorporates both celestial and chthonic/aquatic—that is, afterlife—symbolic motifs, fit for a member of the elite whose soul is preparing to embark upon the treacherous Path of Souls.

Immediately north of Burial 57 is a plot numbered Burial 47, which sits directly east of another northside grave containing the poorly preserved remains of seven people. And just beyond these, located even further toward the north, is another log-lined tomb, cataloged as Burial 38, containing the skeletons of five more elite Natives—these deposited each with a single copper celt and a pair of copper-covered ear spools.

Moreover, four of the individuals in Burial 38 were possessed of many elaborate headdresses comparable to the headgear interred in Burial 57. The fifth corpse, however, although lacking such a headdress, was found with a carved shell gorget and an engraved, scalloped—that is, petaloid—stone palette.[14] Functioning as a sort of portable altar, such stone palettes were a common constituent of Mississippian petacas or sacred bundles, employed for the purpose of consecrating sacrosanct ritual paraphernalia via the holy act of chrismation or anointing. This practice of ceremonial sanctification was accomplished with the use of colorful, spiritually potent pigments and other hallowed substances that served to set apart the particular object of devotion from common, day-to-day items.[15] Clearly, the elite individuals buried beneath the northern terrace—perhaps representing a team of elite ritual specialists—were held in much higher esteem than those deposited in the surrounding flank of the mortuary mound.

It is notable, however, that in a number of burials outside of the northern terrace, one or two petacas were present with the deceased— some of which contained headdresses not worn by the individual but yet buried with him in the form of a sacred bundle. Burial 28, for example, found in the northeast quadrant of Mound C, included a headdress bundle containing a Braden-style eagle copper repoussé plate, a baton hair ornament, a bilobed copper hair ornament, cut tortoiseshell strips, and a stone pipe. What was likely the remains of a second sacred bundle, containing a negative-painted gourd effigy bowl, squash seeds, a copper plate, two human effigy pipes—likely depicting Morning Star in his role as the center of the cosmos—and a square greenstone slab palette with nearby graphite and galena specimens, were also present in Burial 28. The latter of these were used in sacred ceremonies of healing. Burial 30, also in the northeast quadrant, contained evidence of bundling near his head, composed of a scalloped stone palette, red ocher, charcoal, galena, and other pigments. In the northwestern quadrant of Mound C, Burial 44 was found to contain the remains of one or more petacas. These constitute a wide variety of objects, including a number of chunkey stones, pipes, greenstone celts, shell beads, copper-covered wooden beads, and mica. At the feet of the deceased were discovered turtle-shell batons, mica crosses, projectile points, a rectangular scalloped stone palette, a graphite reel, green and red pigments—likely galena and ocher—animal bones, potsherds, stones, clamshells, and two conch shells—possibly for the ceremonial consumption of cassina. Burial 74, located in the southwestern quadrant of the mound, had two sacred bundles—one at his head and another at his feet. The first contained a plain slab palette, a Duck River flint blade attached to two tear-shaped mica ornaments, clay pipe fragment, a fragment of a greenstone celt, potsherds, and animal bones. At his feet was another headdress bundle, consisting of mica crosses, mica disks, fragments of mussel shells, a bone pin, various animal bones, and bird phalanges. Lastly, Burial 109, found in the southeastern quadrant, held the largest and most complex sacred bundle. This cache contained three galena cubes, one galena lump, red pigment on a small, decorated stone palette, copper fragments, a pair of bilobed copper hair ornaments, shark teeth, bits of kaolin, a bone pin fragment, sheet copper eagle claws, sheet-copper-embossed plumes, sheet-copper key-sided (jagged-edged) mace symbol badges, copper-covered ear spools, copper-covered "milkweed pod" wooden rattles, conch shell fragments covered in copper and mica, tortoise-shell crested bird effigy hair ornament, tortoiseshell strips, cut and incised tortoiseshell ornaments, fragments of a copper repoussé plate, and finally a copper-covered wooden disk in the shape of a scalp motif. It is notable that motifs related to the Classic Braden Birdman icon—for example, maces and raptor-related images—were limited primarily to the eastern quarter of Mound C.[16]

As remarkable as all of these burials we've discussed no doubt were, they're arguably still not the most significant of the hundreds of interments recovered from the vicinity of Mound C. That designation would have to go to a pair of individuals hastily deposited in Burial 15—another log-lined grave—positioned on the north side of the eastern ramp that leads up to the summit of the mortuary mound: CSS-059 and CSS-060[17]—whom I affectionately refer to as Peanut and

⊚ ⊚ ⊚

Fig. 5.2. CSS-059 and CSS-060, two statues discovered in Burial 15 at Etowah.
See also color plate 10.

Photograph courtesy of David H. Dye

Peach. Unlike the grouping of plots found within the northern terrace, Burial 15 did not contain the remains of once living human beings, but rather a set of expertly executed male and female white marble statues. Generally associated with ancient Greek culture, marble is probably not the first medium that immediately springs to mind when one thinks of Native North American statuary, assuming one is aware of Amerindian "idols" at all. And yet, Peanut and Peach weren't the only human effigy marble statues to be recovered from Etowah. Although less well preserved, another effigy, serially marked CSS-087, was "found in one of the low mounds now nearly obliterated, to the east of the Great Mound"[18]—that is, in either mound D, E, or F, located just east of Mound A or Temple Mound. While the marble medium is indeed rare, similar statues have been recovered from all over the Mississippi

⊚ ⊚ ⊚

Fig. 5.3. "Sandy" (CSS-033), a statue found at Sellars Farm
in Middle Cumberland. See also color plate 11.

Photograph courtesy of David H. Dye

Valley—especially in the Tennessee-Cumberland region, where some
forty-two similar specimens have been uncovered.[19] Figures such as
these would have been sheltered within the temples and charnel houses
that once stood atop certain of the burial mounds specifically dedicated
to ancestor worship and mortuary practices. But, unlike the flint clay
statuettes from Cahokia that were later drilled to function as ceremonial pipes, these statues do not appear to represent supernatural, nonhuman entities, such as gods or spirits. Often found in mated pairs, it is
more likely that the Etowah effigies stand for ancestral progenitors—or,
at the very least, powerful shaman-like figures shown in a state of deep
trance. Perhaps both may be the case.

The latter possibility is especially evident in CSS-003—known by the nickname, Sandy—a magnificent soft siltstone statue found at Sellars Farm in Middle Cumberland that, as of March 21, 2014, has been officially adopted as Tennessee's state artifact.[20] The execution of this piece clearly exhibits masterful artistry and skill—especially in the expression. The expertly carved facial features convincingly convey an absolute sense of captivation and wonder—and above all, total entrancement. The same may be said of the countenances of Peanut and Peach, both of whom seem to communicate to the viewer states of enchanted bewilderment—but no less mesmerized by whatever it is that they are seeing and experiencing. Art historian Rebecca R. Stone fittingly refers to such ecstatic expressions as "the trance gaze."[21]

> The trance gaze involves eyes that look through, beyond, in, out, but not at something or someone else. . . [Trance] eyes purposely deny entrance, withholding it due to the premium placed on the ineffable and the Not-Here. They positively look Elsewhere. Thus, the trance eye is [. . .] ambiguous, an eye but not a normal one, intentionally mysterious.[22]

Moreover, even the poses of their bodies are suggestive of what American anthropologist Felicitas D. Goodman called shamanic trance postures[23]—āsana-like bodily poses, the adoption of which are prone to induce the generation of various unique trance states. Take Peach, for example, who, as American anthropologists Kevin E. Smith and James V. Miller describe her, "sits in the kneeling position . . . Her hands [. . .] are to the sides of her thighs . . . Her legs are folded back under her body . . ."[24] Compare this Southeastern pose to Goodman's description of that of the so-called Aztec Corn Goddess, which the anthropologist uses as a prime example to explain her concept of shamanic trance postures.

> The Aztecs [. . .] always represented [the Aztec Corn Goddess] as a kneeling young woman sitting on her heels with her outstretched

hands placed gracefully, palms down, on her thighs close to her body. [This] was a posture for changing shape, for metamorphosis. [. . .] If all went well, as if in response to a magic formula, [those in this posture] would slip back into the age of our beginnings, when humans could at will turn into animals and animals could be people.[25]

The similarity between this tried and true shamanic trance posture and the pose of Peach is simply uncanny. Indeed, Goodman may as well be describing the bodily position of CSS-060. Furthermore, in addition to opening inquiries into the crossover between Central and North American Indigenous art and iconography, the possibility that Peach is shown in a posture specifically associated with bestial shapeshifting only increases the probability that such statues were indeed designed to reflect widespread shamanic techniques.

In addition to CSS-059 and CSS-060, Burial 15 also included a number of ceremonial items that, by this point, should be familiar to the reader from our analyses of graves at other MIIS sites. Besides the disarticulated bones of four individuals, these interments incorporated "stone and clay pipes, copper-covered wooden ear discs, fragments of a copper head ornament, a mica disc, a shell pendant, and some red ocher."[26] Notably, some of the pipes recovered from Etowah are decorated with distinctive small, knob-like bumps or protuberances. We'll learn in chapter seven that these "nodes" are indicative of the use of *Datura* spp., and in fact researchers have discovered "a strong signal for tropane, an alkaloid generally associated with plants from the *Datura* genus within the Solanaceae family, jimson weed being a common example," in at least one Southeastern "medicine tube" used for smoking plant matter.[27]

While the specific form has changed, it is evident that the symbolism we encountered in Cahokia and Spiro regarding the mound as axis mundi and its relation to Above and Below World motifs persisted at the Etowah site. Often including marine shell fragments, the grave-riddled flank of Mound C symbolically marked the edges of the Middle World, representing the waters of the Underworld, upon which the mound, typical of the earth, was envisaged as floating. In the later stages of Mound C's construction, it is significant that the summit was left free of burials, where a temple or charnel house—likely equipped with a central fire, connecting, with its column of smoke, the building to the skies—stood for the heavens. But, as archaeologists Johann A. Sawyer and Adam King have rightly argued, "the key link was to the realm of the dead."

> In essence, Mound C was turned into an entrance to the Path of Souls—a path the dead were destined to follow as they traveled to their new homes across the Milky Way.[28]

SIX

THE NECROPOLIS OF MOUNDVILLE

If Picture Cave constituted the conception of the Mississippian peoples and Cahokia amounted to their birth, then Moundville surely may be equated with the opposite end of that spectrum. We have seen how the conceptualization of the cosmos as a three-tiered constitution affected the ways in which the lands utilized by the Mississippians were appropriated—with Birdman and avian imagery being especially concentrated at Cahokia in the north and herpetic iconography related to the Great Serpent dominating at Moundville in the south. The latter, therefore, was very much viewed as a material reflection of the Below World domain—that is, of the chthonic realm ruled by the Great Serpent-Underwater Panther. It is perhaps for this reason that Moundville eventually evolved into a veritable necropolis, with Natives traveling from all over Southeastern North America to deposit the remains of deceased relatives and loved ones within the vicinity of that sacred ceremonial ground. To quote King and Reilly,

> Moundville took on a role as portal to the Path of Souls. Predictably, much of the symbolism prominent at Moundville appears to be related to the rituals of death and the journey along the Path of Souls that was undoubtedly a concern for all Native Americans during the Mississippian period whatever their regional affiliation, just as it is for all human beings of any time or place.[1]

Beginning around 1150 CE, the population at Moundville began to organize itself into a powerful chiefdom, expanding to around thirteen thousand permanent inhabitants, occupying some three hundred acres. A century and a half later, however, for reasons unknown, the Moundville chiefdom transformed into something of a sacred site—specifically concerned with the phenomenology of death and the soul's subsequent navigation of the Path of Souls.[2] In point of fact, while we have encountered clear evidence that the Path of Souls model was present at the other sites discussed herein, the vast majority of the still extant Path of Souls art and iconography came down to us via the site of Moundville. By 1300 CE, Moundville had transitioned into a veritable necropolis, occupied mainly by a religious sodality of shamanic soul specialists, proficient psychopomps whose focus and function was the assistance the souls of the dead in their precarious journeys along the Path of Souls.

We have seen how some Southeastern peoples, such as the Ojibwa or Chippewa, formed secretive medicine societies that were possessed of occult knowledge concerning the fate of the soul and the dangerous journey it must take following physical death—initiated wisdom that was limited solely to those who had been received into the rites of the medicine society. The Midéwiwin, for instance, is known to have had a dual manifestation, the second of which—the Dzhibai' Midéwigân or Ghost Lodge—was concerned solely with funeral rites and with the completion of the perilous Path of Souls cycle. At the necropolis of Moundville, this special formation of the medicine society took precedence, with initiates playing the shamanic role of psychopomp for the deceased, guiding the souls of the dead into the afterlife. In the Great Lakes region, in contradistinction to the orient-occident orientation of the traditional medicine lodge, the Ghost Lodge was situated on a north-south axis, representative of the Path of Souls itself—the Milky Way galaxy—which arched over the earth with its two entrance points being located in the meridional and septentrional quarters.

Indicative of the degrees of the Ghost Society, the lodge of the Dzhibai' Midéwigân was fashioned with four vertical poles along the centerline of the structure. Importantly, evidence of one such building was discovered within the vicinity of the Moundville site, confirming the presence of this particular manifestation of the medicine society among the Alabama Natives. These pillars were often topped with the preserved remains of various species of bird, one for each degree, with the owl referring uniquely to the rites of the Ghost Lodge. Communicating their owners' status as Ghost Lodge initiates, members of the Dzhibai' Midéwigân carried effigies of this creature, called by the onomatopoeic title of Ko-Ko-Ka-O among the Ojibwa, and indeed the remains of actual mummified owls. In what little excavations have been executed at the Moundville site, eight of these carved or sculpted strigine creations have been found.[3] In the sacred birch-bark scrolls of the Southern Ojibwa, Ko-Ko-Ka-O is especially associated with the Path of Souls, envisaged as guiding the souls of shamans and of the dead along

◉ ◉ ◉

Fig. 6.1. Owl effigy bowl.

Photo by the author

◎ ◎ ◎

Fig. 6.2. Owl is closely connected to the "Path of Souls" mythology.
See also color plate 4.

Illustration by A. Rivero; Vix Volante Creative

the Milky Way galaxy. For, according to the Anishinaabe, the Owl
Manitou was the only supernatural that was specially equipped with
the magical means of successfully navigating the afterlife journey.[4] "An
owl summons the dead and becomes a relative, a grandfather," Pomedli

explains, "who mediates between life and death and who guides by loaning its eyes to travelers on the path to a new home."[5]

According to Ojibwa lore, Ko-Ko-Ka-O was originally possessed of two sets of eyes, one of which provided him with the ability to see in the darkness of the realm of the deceased. In one tale about Owl's special eyesight, the strigine Manitou is being chased by Myeengun—the Wolf Manitou. After being placed in an underworld, cave-like hole by Myeengun, Nanabozho—Rabbit—spits the visionary juice of the tobacco plant into Ko-Ko-Ka-O's eyes, blinding him to the sight of Middle World objects while forcing him to open his eyes as wide as possible, providing him with a more subtle type of sight. As Wilbert observes, the ordeal of depositing tobacco juice in the eyes of shamans is possessed of both magical and initiatory functions.

> Tobacco is [. . .] clearly experienced as a sight- and vision-altering drug that permits the tobacco shaman to behold the numinous world. To obtain visionary eyes of this kind, shamanic neophytes [. . .] must submit to the painful ordeal of having their sight changed through the external application of tobacco juice directly on the eye. As explained by the Indians of the Upper Amazon, this procedure is believed to make the novice shaman clear-sighted for the new world in which he has chosen to live . . .
>
> External application of tobacco to the eye has an initiatory purpose in a different context as well. Uninitiated eyes of travelers to unknown regions must be protected from spirit intrusion. Spirits are variously considered to inhabit rocks, hills, mountains, rapids, and similar landmarks. To prevent them from entering the body and the mind of the inexperienced traveler, tobacco juice is poured into his eyes to change them from vulnerable normal organs to eyes fit to behold the numen.[6]

The above story may have served as a charter for shamanic rites of passage among the Ojibwa. Another tale tells a different story about Owl's special sight. Ko-Ko-Ka-O loans his eyes to Nanabozho so that the latter might have vision while visiting Myeengun, who was the first created entity to experience death and the guardian of the realm of the dead—in the Below World.[7] Ko-Ko-Ka-O is therefore particularly pertinent in regard to the ability of the visionary shamans at Moundville to guide those without this special initiated knowledge (i.e., the "blind") along the treacherous Path of Souls. The shaman playing the role of psychopomp in effect became Owl in relation to the soul of the deceased. Much of the art and iconography discovered at Moundville pertains specifically to this hidden wisdom.

Besides the owl, there are at least five images that prevail at Moundville and are closely related to the Path of Souls cycle: bones, skulls, winged serpents, the so-called "hand-and-eye" motif, and raptors. Of those five, the hand-and-eye motif and the winged serpent are by far the most prevalent, appearing thirty-one and thirty-three times, respectively. In at least twenty examples, the hand-and-eye motif is found alone, but seven times it is shown alongside images of bones, while its appearance with skulls is limited to just two depictions—these latter combinations highlighting a special affinity of the hand-and-eye motif with notions of death and the soul. Only once is it conjoined with the winged serpent—the latter appearing solo in every other instance. In another single example, the hand and eye is combined with the form of the raptor. Eleven times, however, the raptor alone is depicted on the vessel. Finally, while neither of them appears solo in any case, bones and skulls pop up together on three known vessels.[8]

First and foremost, as I wrote above, the presence of osseous and cranial imagery in conjunction with iconography uniquely related to the Path of Souls cycle is a clear indication that the symbols in this set are specifically related to a postmortem rite of passage. Particularly, the bones and skulls correspond to the binary conceptualization of the Amerindian soul, ascribed to by a number of tribes in the Southeast. According to this model, individual bones, especially those depicted as being fractured, indicate what some tribes referred to as the life-soul—a mindless aspect of the soul that is said to be fixed or earthbound, the function of which is to supply an individual with vitality, not unlike a battery.

⊙ Plate 1. Otter is an important supernatural in the Ojibwa cosmology.
ILLUSTRATION BY A. RIVERO; VIX VOLANTE CREATIVE

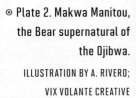

⊙ Plate 2. Makwa Manitou, the Bear supernatural of the Ojibwa.
ILLUSTRATION BY A. RIVERO; VIX VOLANTE CREATIVE

⊙ Plate 3. Identified as the "tobacco moth," *Manduca sexta*, Mothra or Mothman is a Mississippian supernatural specifically associated with *Datura* and *Nicotiana* spp.

ILLUSTRATION BY A. RIVERO; VIX VOLANTE CREATIVE

⊙ Plate 4. Owl is closely connected to the "Path of Souls" mythology.

ILLUSTRATION BY A. RIVERO; VIX VOLANTE CREATIVE

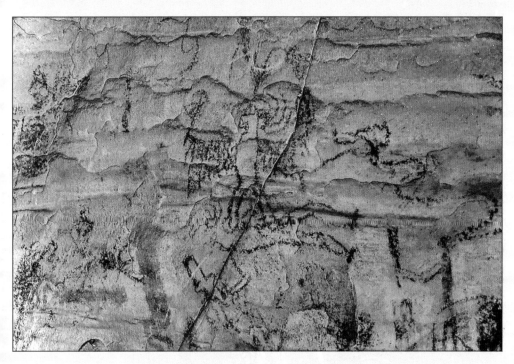

Plate 5. A depiction of a death rite, found in Picture Cave,
officiated by a shaman dressed as a bird.
PHOTO BY THE AUTHOR

Plate 6. Red Horn or Morning Star, as he appears in Picture Cave.
PHOTO BY THE AUTHOR

Plate 7. The Hero Twins as depicted on the wall of Picture Cave.

PHOTO BY THE AUTHOR

Plate 8. The Great Serpent, as depicted in Picture Cave.

PHOTO BY THE AUTHOR

◉ Plate 9. A figure falling headfirst from a ladder, found in Picture Cave.

PHOTO BY THE AUTHOR

◉ Plate 10. CSS-059 and
CSS-060, two statues
discovered in Burial 15
at Etowah.
PHOTOGRAPH COURTESY OF
DAVID H. DYE

⊙ Plate 11. "Sandy" (CSS-033), a statue found at Sellars Farm in Middle Cumberland.
PHOTOGRAPH COURTESY OF DAVID H. DYE

⊙ Plate 12. The Rattlesnake Disk, found in Moundville, shows imagery connected to the Path of Souls mythology.
PHOTOGRAPH COURTESY OF DAVID H. DYE

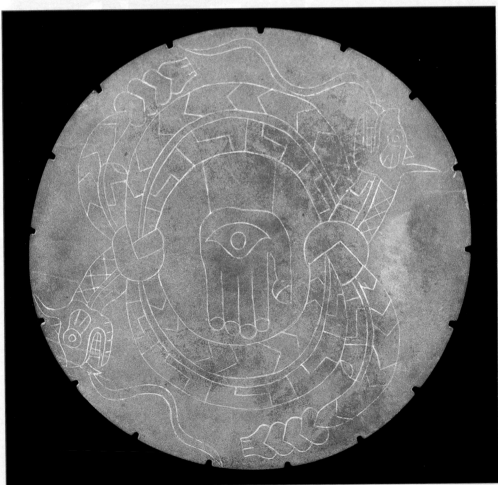

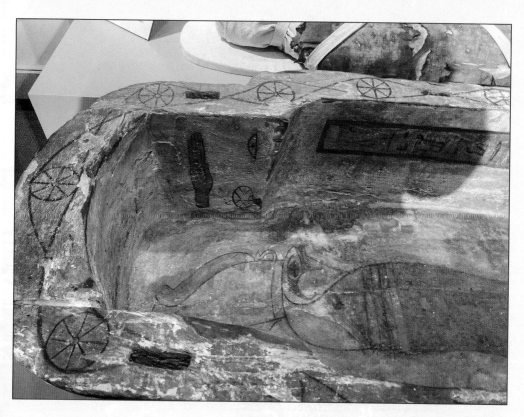

⊙ Plates 13 and 14. The coffin of Tchaenhotep, who lived between 3,093 BP and 2,688 BP and was buried in Ta-Set-Neferu, the "Valley of the Queens." Currently housed at the Kentucky Science Center of Louisville, the markings on her coffin bear a number of striking similarities to the iconography of the MIIS.

PHOTOS BY THE AUTHOR

⊚ Plate 15. The Willoughby Disk was recovered from Moundville and depicts iconography closely associated with the Path of Souls.

PHOTO BY DADEROT

⊚ Plate 16. A "Spaghetti style" gorget, carved from shell, depicting a figure submerged in a boiling pot, surrounded by twisting objects reminiscent of roots.

PHOTO BY HERB ROE

Even after death, this part of the soul remains in matter, where the life energy it once supplied to a living person is recycled and returned to the earth, repurposed perhaps for one's living descendants. Skulls, on the other hand, signify something known as the free-soul—the potentially immortal aspect of the soul that is volatile or mobile, its function being to animate the physical body. It is the part of the soul that is *free* to wander about during dreams and out-of-body and near-death experiences, and as such it is the vehicle that carries one's consciousness, thoughts, and feelings forward following the fatality of the physical frame. Oftentimes, in the form of a flame, a feather, a tongue, or an arrow, the free-soul is shown emerging from the open mouths of skulls and, more rarely, from the splintered fractures of broken bones.[9] The arrow is especially applicable because, when the soul projects itself toward the ogee in the Chief's Hand constellation, it does so in the form of a launched arrow. There are a number of mythological charters that support this supposition, two of which we shall recount below. Personally, it is helpful for me to think of the life-soul as one's genetic makeup—which obviously must remain behind for the benefit of one's genetic descendants—and of the free-soul as one's individual psyche. It is easy to see how both of these may be said to constitute one's "self."

The Great Serpent, then, is possessed of a dual manifestation: the Winged or Feathered Serpent and the Underwater Panther. While there are obvious similarities between them, one would be incorrect to interpret the Great Serpent, on account of his feathered form, as an avatar or type of the feathered serpent Quetzalcoatl—an Aztec deity representative of the planet Venus. If there is any historical affinity between these two supernatural entities, insofar as their temperaments are totally at odds with one another, it would at best constitute an extreme example of enantiodromia—what Nietzsche called transvaluation, where the character of a given subject or object has taken on completely different, often opposite, qualities. A perfect illustration is the fact that the Great Serpent of the MIIS represents the constellation recognized by most Westerners as Scorpius. Quetzalcoatl, as I have said, has a uniquely venereal or Venusian quality.

Appearing alone on no less than thirty-two vessels, the Great Serpent is believed to be the guardian of the Below World. How a Below World supernatural may also be said to be a constellation requires some explanation. To many of the Southeastern Natives, the Below World was literally understood to be the star-studded night sky, which rotates to the heavens every twelve hours or so, physically changing places with the blue skies of day. When the Below World is occupying the heavens at night, the Great Serpent assumes his form as the Feathered Serpent, policing the skies for any uninitiated free-soul attempting to traverse the Path of Souls. During the daylight hours, on the other hand, when the twinkling Below World returns to its natural, basic position, the Great Serpent then sheds his feathers and wings, transforming into the terrible Underwater Panther—a fearsome entity comparable to the Judeo-Christian conceptualization of Lucifer. This is one reason why tales of the spirits—and especially of the Great Serpent—are told only during wintertime. In summertime, Scorpius is always visible in the night sky, and therefore he may potentially overhear anything said in regard to him. On winter nights, however, the constellation of the scorpion never ascends above the horizon, remaining in the Below World all winter long, like a hibernating bear, in his manifestation as the Underwater Panther. In an entirely different context, which will be explored in depth below, the Great Serpent alludes to the intoxicating larva of the *Manduca sexta* moth—commonly referred to as the "tobacco hornworm."

Although it appears incised upon at least thirty-one examples of Hemphill pots and vessels, arguably the most important examples of the hand-and-eye motif are found upon two expertly carved stone palettes, used both as portable altars for sacred bundles and as consecrated surfaces for mixing ceremonial substances and special pigments. It is possible that they were employed in some instances for the preparation of sacred medicines specifically designed to induce an encounter with certain supernaturals residing upon the Path of Souls. We'll learn more about such psychedelic—that is, soul manifesting—substances in a later chapter.

The first of these is a sandstone palette known as the Rattlesnake

Disk that shows the hand-and-eye motif, inverted, surrounded by two tie-snakes. We have already seen that the hand alludes to what many North American Natives understand to be the Chief's Hand constellation, which most Westerners would recognize as the constellation of Orion. There are a couple of interesting mythological charters that explain how this "hand star" came to be. "Spring-boy was captured by the chief of the sky village, Long Arm," according to the Mandan version of the Lodge-Boy and Thrown-Away story, "but his brother Lodge-boy rescued him in the form of a spider." As they fled toward the hole in the sky through which they would escape and return to earth,

> Long Arm went and placed his hand over the hole by which they passed through so as to catch them. Spring-boy made a motion with the hatchet as if to cut it off at the wrist and said, "This second time your hand has committed a crime, and it shall be a sign to the people on earth." So it is today that we see the hand in the heavens. The white people call it Orion. The belt is where they cut across the wrist, the thumb and fingers also show; they are hanging down like a hand. "The hand star" it is called.[10]

In the version taught by the Crow peoples,

> [The Hero Twin] thought about it and he figured that it must have been Baaáalichke [One with a Long Arm] who took [his brother]. He looked to the sky and saw a hole. He then shot his arrows and where his arrows went he went. When he got to the sky, he found a camp and life there . . . Baaáalichke dropped the twin, Thrown Behind the Tipi Lining helped his twin up and put him on his shoulder and took him to the opening in the sky. He threw his arrows, which took them back to earth.
>
> Thrown Behind the Tipi Lining put his brother down on the ground. Then Baaáalichke reached down from the sky and tried to pick up Thrown Into the Spring, but Thrown Into the Spring cut the hand off at the wrist and it hit the ground, then Thrown

into the Spring threw the hand back to the sky where it became the Hand Star. Thrown into the Spring said, "You will no longer eat or destroy others. Your hand in the sky will be a symbol for all time of your cruelty." And this is how the Hand Star came to be.[11]

The eye, on the other hand, or the "ogee" that is in fact a mégis shell held in the palm—just as they're held by members of the Midéwiwin in the Great Lakes region—signifies Messier 42, aka the Orion Nebula, envisaged by the MIIS as being an entry point onto the Path of Souls. A tale from the Blackfeet tells us how this ogee portal came to be.

One day a young woman was in the woods gathering firewood. Looking up into the sky she spotted a star. She wished she was married to this star. When she was again in the woods gathering firewood, a man approached her. He told her that he had heard her wish and wanted her to go with him. She agreed. Upon agreeing she had to close her eyes, and when she opened them, she was with her new husband in the sky. He had one request, which was that she not pull out a turnip that was planted in the garden no matter if it was in the way. Her curiosity got the best of her one day, and she pulled the turnip out of the ground leaving a gaping hole. When she looked through the hole, she saw her home and family and immediately started to cry. She wanted to go back home. Her husband granted her wish once more, and she returned home.[12]

For the Iroquoian peoples who lived in the Allegheny and northern Susquehanna valleys, bark from the roots of the *arbor mundi* or "world tree" replaces the forbidden Blackfeet turnip.

In the Sky-World there was a man who had a wife, and the wife was expecting a child. The woman became hungry for all kinds of strange delicacies, as women do when they are with child. She kept her husband busy almost to distraction finding delicious things for her to eat.

○ ○ ○

Fig. 6.3. The Rattlesnake Disk, found in Moundville, shows imagery
connected to the Path of Souls mythology. See also color plate 12.
Photograph courtesy of David H. Dye

In the middle of the Sky-World there was a Great Tree which was
not like any of the trees we know. It was tremendous; it had grown
there forever. It had enormous roots that spread out from the floor
of the Sky-World. . . . The tree was not supposed to be marked or
mutilated by any of the beings who dwelt in the Sky-World. It was a
sacred tree that stood at the center of the universe.

The woman decided that she wanted some bark from one of the
roots of the Great Tree—perhaps as a food or as a medicine, we

don't know. She told her husband this. He didn't like the idea. He knew it was wrong. But she insisted, and he gave in. So he dug a hole among the roots of this great sky tree, and he bared some of its roots. But the floor of the Sky-World wasn't very thick, and he broke a hole through it. He was terrified, for he had never expected to find empty space underneath the world.

But his wife was filled with curiosity. He wouldn't get any of the roots for her, so she set out to do it herself. She bent over and she looked down, and she saw the ocean far below. . . . No one knows just what happened next. Some say she slipped. Some say her husband, fed up with all the demands she had made on him, pushed her.

So she fell through the hole. As she fell, she frantically grabbed at its edges, but her hands slipped. However, between her fingers there clung bits of things that were growing on the floor of the Sky-World and bits of the root tips of the Great Tree. And so she began to fall toward the great ocean far below.[13]

As we shall see shortly, the motif of bark from the roots of a Great Tree is significant for my *Missihuasca* hypothesis, discussed below. For it is in the bark of the roots of many entheogenic *Acacia* species that the potent psychedelic molecule N,N-DMT is most concentrated. But I'm getting ahead of myself. We'll return to this topic in chapter eight.

Surrounding this hand-and-eye glyph on the Rattlesnake Disk are two caduceus-like tie-snakes, entwined about one another, encircling the hand in what closely resembles a Native American answer to the ancient Egyptian symbol of the Ouroboros. These tie-snakes, I will venture to say, allude to the dual arches of the Milky Way galaxy—one above and the other beneath the Earth. Evidence for this latter position will be cited below.

One thing I find interesting about this icon is its similarity to ancient metaphysical models of astronomy appearing halfway around the planet, in areas such as ancient Greece, Egypt, and even Babylon. In the ancient Greek model, for instance, the intersection of the Milky Way with the ecliptic—which follows the wheel of the zodiac—creates something known in Platonic circles as Plato's X, described by the Athenian philosopher himself in his book *Timaeus* and representing the *anima mundi* or World Soul. At least since the time of Pythagoras and the Presocratics, the Milky Way was imagined as the place where souls, before and after incarnation, reside, constantly orbiting the galaxy in the way that souls—according to Plato—are wont to do. In his surreal work, "Dream of Scipio," Roman philosopher Cicero instructs:

> "This sort of [virtuous] life is your passport into the sky, to a union with those who have finished their lives on earth and who, upon being released from their bodies, inhabit that place at which you are now looking" (it was a circle or surpassing brilliance gleaming out amidst the blazing stars), "which takes its name, the Milky Way, from the Greek word."[14]

The Tyrian Neoplatonist Porphyry explains in his work *On the Cave of the Nymphs* that at the two points where the Milky Way and the ecliptic intersect are found a pair of occluded portals or gates—one in the north and the other in the south. The first, the Tyrian says, is where disincarnate souls enter our solar system for the purpose of acquiring a body and being born, while the second constitutes the exit point used by discorporate souls—called gods by Porphyry—that have completed an individual round of incarnation. The first-century Roman poet Marcus Manilius correctly identifies the positions of these two points of intersection.

> Nor does it [the Zodiac] elude the sight of the eye, as if it were a circle to be comprehended by the mind alone, even as the previous circles [equatorial, tropical, etc.] are perceived by the mind; nay, throughout its mighty circuit it shines like a baldric studded with stars and gives brilliance to heaven with its broad outline standing out in sharp relief. The other circle [the Milky Way] is placed crosswise to it [. . .] passing between the blazing tail of the Scorpion and the tip of the Archer's left hand and arrow . . . [and by] the Twins through the bottom of their sign . . .[15]

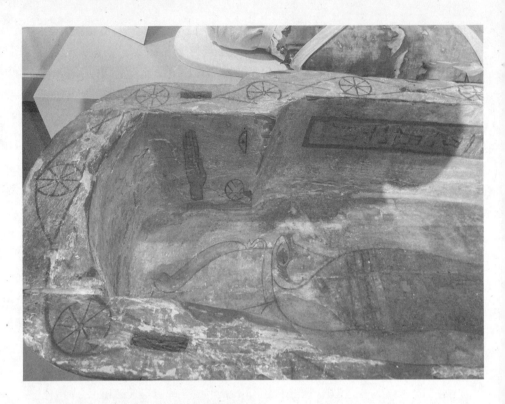

◉ ◉ ◉

Fig. 6.4. The coffin of Tchaenhotep, who lived between 3,093 BP and 2,688 BP and was buried in Ta-Set-Neferu, the "Valley of the Queens." Currently housed at the Kentucky Science Center of Louisville, the markings on her coffin bear a number of striking similarities to the iconography of the MIIS. See also color plates 13 and 14.

Photos by the author

Next to the Twins or Gemini is the sign of the Bull—Taurus—and before them both stands the constellation of the Hunter, Orion—also known as the Hand Star.

In the Egyptian system, the Milky Way is the star-studded, arching body of the goddess Nuit referred to in the *Pyramid Texts* as the Street of Stars. Along this stellar street the pharaoh must journey if he is to reach *Sekhet-A'aru*—the Field of Rushes:

> The Castle of the Mace of the Great Ones will not oppose me on the Street of Stars. Behold, I have reached the height of heaven . . . —Utterance 262

> Behold, I have come and gone, for I have reached the height of the sky, and I have not been opposed by the Great Ones of the Castle of the Mace, who are on the Milky Way. —Utterance 475[16]

According to the *Pyramid Texts*—namely, the inscriptions in the tomb of the pharaoh Unas—Orion, which is recognized by the architects of Unas's tomb as Osiris, is the area at which the soul, assuming the "godform" of Osiris, meets this Street of Stars, leading the soul directly into the *Duat*—the Egyptian conceptualization of the underworld.

> In your name of Dweller in Orion, with a season in the sky and a season on earth. O Osiris, turn your face and look on this King, for your seed which issued from you is effective . . . —Utterance 219

> The Netherworld has grasped your hand at the place where Orion is. —Utterance 437

> Behold, he has come as Orion, behold, Osiris has come as Orion . . . —Utterance 442

> O King, you are this great star, the companion of Orion, who traverses the sky with Orion, who navigates the Netherworld with Osiris . . . —Utterance 466

May a stairway to the Netherworld be set up for you in the place where Orion is. —Utterance 610

You shall reach the sky as Orion. —Utterance 723

I have gone upon the ladder with my foot on Orion. —Utterance 1763

May Orion give me his hand. —Utterance 1561[17]

Even in the Papyrus of Ani, better known as the Egyptian Book of the Dead, this tradition continues unaltered. In spells 72 and 176, we find, for example:

The Milky Way will not reject me, the rebels will not have power over me, I shall not be turned away from your portals, the doors shall not be closed against me . . . —Spell 72

⊙ ⊙ ⊙

Fig. 6.5. The Great Serpent, as depicted in Picture Cave. See also color plate 8.

Photo by the author

I will not enter the place of destruction, none shall bring me offer-
ings of what the gods detest, because I pass pure into the midst of
the Milky Way . . . —Spell 176[18]

In the Babylonian model, however, it isn't Orion that is named, but
rather the constellation located just behind him, which we would recognize as the sign of Taurus—right next to Manilius's Twins. The other
entrance point, at the opposite end of the galaxy where the Milky Way
intersects with the ecliptic a second time, is in the vicinity of Scorpio—
precisely where the MIIS places the Great Serpent. Significantly, for the
Babylonian astrologers, there are two gates of Utu or Shammash—the
sun god—in the heavens. In the cylinder texts used by these ancient
sky-gazers, one of those gates is guarded by bovine figures—the other
being protected by giant scorpions. In the Babylonian *Epic of Gilgamesh*,
from 1100 BCE, we read:

[Gilgamesh] came to the mountains whose name is Mashu;
approached the twin peaks which guard each day the coming and
going of Shamash [the Sun god]. Their tops reach the vault of
heaven; below their feet touch the underworld [Kur]. Scorpion-
people guard the gate . . .[19]

In their book, *Gods, Demons and Symbols of Ancient Mesopotamia*, British
historians Jeremy Black and Anthony Green add: "In the art of the Old
Babylonian and Kassite Periods, the bull-man appears [. . .] as an atten-
dant of the sun god, Shamash . . ."[20] Similarly, the former curator at the
British Museum in London Dominique Collon tells us: "One popular
scene shows [. . .] a god with couchant bull supporting a winged gate."[21]
The Milky Way, conversely, is represented by the body of an enormous
serpent—not to be confused with the Great Serpent of the MIIS—shown
winding its way around *kudurrus* in a manner reminiscent of the two tie-
snakes depicted upon Moundville's Rattlesnake Disk. Archaeoastronomer
George Latura Beke elaborates in his amazing monograph *Visible Gates in
the Pagan Skies*:

On Babylonian kudurrus, or land-grant monuments (c. 1100 BC), we repeatedly see the symbols of the Sun, the Moon, and Venus at the top, indicating the Ecliptic, the course of these celestial bodies. Also, we often find a giant serpent [. . .] undulating up the side of the kudurru, and intersecting the Ecliptic, the path of the Sun, Moon, and Venus. The celestial serpent would seem to represent the Milky Way, which intersects the Ecliptic in the night sky.[22]

Beke continues:

With the Ecliptic and the Milky Way repeatedly depicted on Babylonian kudurrus, we should also see symbols for the constellations that mark their intersections, and in fact we often find scorpions (Scorpius) in the bottom register, pointing to that intersection. At the top, the symbols of the high gods Anu and Enlil (and sometimes Ea) appear as shrines topped by a crown of stacked bull-horns, the symbol of divinity throughout Mesopotamian art. If the bull-horn crown is related to the constellation Taurus (as is the case with the Bull of Heaven, the bull-man, the bull with the winged gate), then we have all the ingredients needed to identify the intersections of the celestial circles (Ecliptic and Milky Way), as marked by the constellations Scorpius and Taurus.[23]

The similarities are simply uncanny. Assuming that this model of interpretation continues and crosses over into North America, it is clear that what we're looking at in the case of the Rattlesnake Disk is a depiction of the southern entry point upon the Path of Souls, surrounded by a herpetic representation of the Milky Way galaxy. This very formula appears even in Mayan iconography, with the place of creation being this same intersection, understood by the Maya to be the constellation of a turtle having three stars (Orion's belt and the wrist of the Chief's Hand) upon his shell, near where the ecliptic meets the Milky Way galaxy. For the ancient Maya, this chelonian portal leads directly onto the "the White Road," which is a clear reference to what the Mississippians envisage as

⊙ ⊙ ⊙

Fig. 6.6. The Willoughby Disk was recovered from Moundville and depicts iconography
closely associated with the Path of Souls. See also color plate 15.
Photo by Daderot

the Path of Souls—called by the Egyptians the Street of Stars.

The second Moundville palette that concerns us here is known as
the Willoughby Disk, the only Moundville palette carved from slate—
as opposed to the more common sandstone. Far more complex than the
image illustrating the Rattlesnake Disk, this slate palette shows two
averse hand-and-eye motifs—presumably one for each threshold occupying the intersections of the Milky Way with the ecliptic—located
in the upper righthand register of this amazing artifact. Below these

appears a depiction of something called a bilobed arrow, with its point indicating the hand situated on the viewer's right. It is as if the craftsman were communicating which of the two celestial gates the free-soul could safely enter—the one located on the right being the southern-winter gate and the other being protected by the Great Serpent entity. Furthermore, recall that it is in the form of an arrow that the free-soul is said to launch itself at the mégis-ogee. Lankford tells us, for instance, that the myths of various Native peoples, "speak of heroic figures who are able to fly through the air or up to the sky by transforming themselves into [. . .] arrows."[24] In another example, the supernatural figure of Red Horn is able to defeat the warrior spirit, Turtle, in a foot race, "after repeatedly projecting himself forward as an arrow."[25]

To the far left of the Willoughby Disk, we find what appears to be an abstract, surrealistic image, which archaeologists in the past have simply referred to as a phantasmagoria—meaning they had no idea what it represented. However, once Reilly began organizing the Mississippian Iconographic Conference at Texas State University in 1992, which involved academics, enthusiasts, and Indigenous alike, it wasn't long before some of the Native Americans present declared that they knew precisely what the "phantasm" was: a stylization of a special species of moth—known as the tobacco moth—the significance of which will be explored in depth below. Separating the pair of hand-and-eye motifs and the bilobed arrow from the stylized tobacco moth on the Willoughby Disk is an elongated, twisted petaca or sacred bundle, embellished by two skulls—potentially signifying the life- and free-soul—peering in opposing directions: one at the moth, the other at the dual hand-and-eye motif and bilobed arrow, as if to imply a close connection between this insect, the soul, and the Land of the Dead.

The inclusion of the tobacco moth, which, as we'll see in the following chapter, is a clear indication of the ceremonial use of both *Nicotiana* spp. and *Datura* spp., raises the question of the identification and function of these stone palettes. Hohokam burial caches in Arizona are known to have held similar palettes—only, in their case, these artifacts are identified not as portable altars or painters' palettes but as snuff trays, used for the purpose of insufflating drugs. The act of snuffing hallucinogens is common in both Central and South America, as well as in Chile and Costa Rica. Moreover, *Datura* spp. and tobacco constitute ideal candidates for the preparations of powdered snuffs. American anthropologist Sean M. Rafferty writes,

> Often interpreted as pigment processing artifacts (many show pigment residue), this need not preclude use as snuff trays as well. They could have multiple uses, and pigments are often applied to give symbolic power to objects. Also, some pigments, which include heavy metals such as manganese, can be neurotoxic, causing hallucinations themselves.[26]

We will return to the topic of *Datura* spp. below.

The raptor theme appears on sixteen Moundville artifacts, on eleven of which it is the sole depiction. Notably, one instance pairs the raptor with the hand-and-eye motif, indicating the congruence of these two familial icons.[27] In contradistinction to the feather-crested, straight-billed Crested Bird motif, which also makes an appearance on several artifacts of the MIIS in allusion to the four Thunders or Winds, the raptor appears on Moundville pottery instead with a uniquely jagged crest of feathers and a hooked, pointed beak, and bearing the characteristic forked eye motif so typical of this supernatural entity. The reader will recall that this forked eye motif is indicative of the constellation Cygnus, whose bright eye—the star Deneb—is located precisely at the fork found at the dark rift of the Milky Way galaxy.

While still serving "as a status or achievement indicator," displaying the degree or grade the individual bearing the badge had attained in the Moundville medicine society, of all the different symbols left to us by the Mississippians, the iconography of the raptor is arguably the most difficult to provide a complete account for. This is due largely to the wide variety of applications of this versatile emblem across the various MIIS sites. At Etowah, for instance, the raptor images, worn exclusively by the elite, served as social indicators of power and prestige—not necessarily initiation.[28] In the necropolis of Moundville, however, divorced from the direct connection to the elite ruling class, the raptor symbol evolved into a mortuary figure known as the Raptor on the Path—an impartial judge who decided the fate of the free-soul approaching the end of the Path of Souls cycle.

Aligned with a figure called Brain Taker or Knocks-a-hole-in-the-head by the Sauk, known as Pierce-head by the Iroquois and the Huron, and labeled Brain-smasher by the Ojibwa, the Winnebago, and others, the function of the Raptor on the Path was to totally obliterate the identity of the free-soul who receives from the Raptor an unfavorable judgment. According to the Sauk, for example, "the fleeting spirit must be swift indeed to avoid having his brains dashed out. If this happens, he is destroyed or lost forever." Similarly, early Jesuit missionaries recorded identical accounts from the Iroquois and Huron, who said that Pierce-head "draws the brains out of the heads of the dead, and keeps them." Ethnographer William Byrd learned at a Saponi mortuary ritual that those judged unfavorably at the fork in the Path are sent by a "buzzard to the bad land." Perhaps to protect the dead from just such a condemning ruling, among the Alabama "a knife is said to have been put into the hand of an Alabama Indian with which to fight an eagle supposed to beset the spirit trail"—the spirit trail being another title for the Path of Souls. Note that, like the vulture and buzzard, the eagle is another type of raptor. Finally, Seminole burial practices:

> included a piece of burnt wood and bow in the left hand, with an arrow held by the right. The fires at the head and feet, as well as the waving of the torches, were to guard him from the approach of "evil birds" who would harm him. [. . .] The piece of burnt wood in his hand was to protect him from the "bad birds" while he was on his skyward journey. These "evil birds" are called Ta-lak-i-çlak-o.[29]

Put simply by Lankford, Brain-smasher's task "is to destroy memory (and humanity?) by removing or smashing the brain." Recall that the Spirit Lodge, secreted away inside of Craig Mound at Spiro, contained

◉ ◉ ◉

Fig. 6.7. A figure falling headfirst from a ladder, found in Picture Cave.
See also color plate 9.

Photo by the author

a copper-covered pipe depicting just such a raptor, perched and feeding upon a severed human head.

Dating back some 12,000 years BP, the imagery of raptors taking the heads of dead humans is among the oldest iconography in the world. At Çatalhüyük, for instance, which is found in southern Anatolia and over 9,500 years old, the so-called Vulture Shrine fresco shows headless bodies, as well as bodiless heads, being carried up (or down) what appears to be a tall staircase connected to a scaffolding—likely an ancient bier-like structure used for something known as a sky burial, wherein vultures were permitted to deflesh corpses, carrying their bodies, bite by bite, into the celestial domain of the Sky World. Strikingly, I found a nearly identical pictograph, revealing a figure falling headfirst from what appears to be a ladder leading to the sky, sketched upon the main panel in Picture Cave. Something similar appears on Pillar 43 at Göbekli Tepe in southeastern Anatolia, dated to around 9,500 BC—some two millennia older than Çatalhüyük—where a vulture is depicted in the act of elevating an imperfect sphere—likely indicative of a human head—into the Sky World. Recall that, for the MIIS, the head or skull could serve as a symbol for the free-soul. Similar iconography, showing a sphere clutched in the talons of a giant raptor, was left behind by the pre-Mississippian Hopewell Indians. Significantly, just below this carved raptor at Göbekli Tepe is a line, indicating the horizon, and below that line is seen an unmistakable carving of a giant scorpion. Could these be early executions of Scorpius—the Great Serpent, who remains below the horizon in the winter—and Cygnus—the Raptor on the Path who lives at the "top of the sky," barring or allowing souls to pass on to the Land of the Dead—etched into stone at Göbekli Tepe? In the author's opinion, it is indeed not out of the realm of possibility that what we're looking at in the case of Pillar 43 is an archaic depiction of the same or a similar Path of Souls model, detectable also in the astro-mythological models of Ancient Babylon, Egypt, Greece, the Maya, and Southeastern North America.

This corpus of five distinctive illustrative icons—bones, skulls, winged serpents, the so-called "hand-and-eye" motif, and raptors—constitutes, therefore, a curious complex of very closely related concepts for the Moundville necropolis, and indeed for the entire Mississippian Ideological Interaction Sphere, that is specifically related to the afterlife model known to the Woodland and Plains Indians as the Path of Souls.[30]

SEVEN

MAGIC PLANTS AND SHAMANISM IN THE MIIS

In the introduction of this book, Reilly was quoted as hypothesizing that each of the Path of Souls vessels probably "contained powerful medicine that would assist the soul of the deceased on the path to overcome the tribulations that the supernatural entity engraved on the bottle represents"—that the images decorating the vessels, moreover, likely "identified the medicine it contained, while linking it with specific rituals that this supernatural controlled."[1] At the time that Reilly made this astute proposal, he couldn't have known that a mere decade later his hypothesis would be proven by a team of talented researchers who, using traditional water-based sonicator and burr sampling methods of mass spectrometry, tested the absorbed residues of fifty-five pottery vessels and eighteen marine shell cups from western Mexico and the American Southeast in search of evidence of prehistoric use of entheogenic plants, and found proof that substances such as *Datura* spp. were indeed being exploited by Native Americans—including the Mississippian Ideological Interaction Sphere.[2]

Of the fifty-five pottery vessels tested by the research team, nearly a quarter of the chosen specimens proved to be positive for the presence of *Datura* alkaloids. As Reilly anticipated, the threatening image of the Great Serpent decorated the face of some of those vessels, such as a Walls Engraved bottle, cataloged GM 5425–824 and housed at the

⊙ ⊙ ⊙

Fig. 7.1. *Datura* spp. played a
significant role in the shamanic
practices of the MIIS.
Photo courtesy of Dion Sanchez

Gilcrease Museum in Tulsa, Oklahoma. Centered on the base of this
skillful artifact is shown a swastika-like swirl-cross or fylfot cross surrounded by ripples of expanding concentric rings, a design that con-
nects the vessel and its contents to the malevolent world below—the
swirl cross being indicative of a whirlpool-like portal that pulls a person
into the chthonic realm.[3] As we shall see, the unifying factor among all
of the *Datura*-positive pottery is an undeniable correlation to the prem-
ises of the Underworld.

Another *Datura*-tainted pottery vessel found was in the form of a
female effigy bottle, known variously as the Earth Mother,[4] the Old-
Woman-Who-Never-Dies,[5] and the Woman in the Patterned Shawl.[6]
Specifically related to the Below World, like the *Datura* flower itself—
which blooms during the night—this hunchbacked crone is often identified with the waxing and waning nocturnal luminary. Consistently
shown kneeling in a short, uniquely patterned, knee-length skirt, this
aged supernatural tends to sport an easily identifiable "bumpy" hair-
style that has the curious distinctive feature of multiple small, knobs—

⊚ ⊚ ⊚
Fig. 7.2 and Fig. 7.3. Noded pots.
Photos by the author

⊚ ⊚ ⊚
**Fig. 7.4. Hunchback
effigy bottles.**
Photo by the author

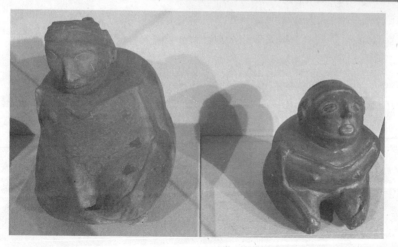

thought to represent the protruding nodes of *Datura* spp. seedpods.[7] Indeed, there is an entire genre of Native American pottery, including Banks Noded, Fortune Noded, Moore Noded, and Southwestern Noded,[8] that is characterized by these strange and unique nodes. According to archaeologists, such vessels are designed specifically to reflect *Datura*'s prickly, unmistakable seedpod. In an important set of articles for *The Arkansas Archaeologist*, for instance, following the lead of VanPool et al., Lankford informs us that "the noded décor creates effigies of the seedpods of Datura, and [. . .] the vessel thus stands as archaeological markers for [. . .] the practice of Datura shamanism . . ."[9] Ergo, it is not surprising that the knob-headed Earth Mother effigy bottle, which may be said to be a variation or type of noded vessel, should contain evidence of having held concoctions involving this particular intoxicating nightshade. Noded pipes have also been recovered from Etowah, indicating that *Datura* spp. weren't just imbibed—but also smoked.[10] Significantly, among the Mixe of Oaxaca, *Datura stramonium* is believed to contain the spirit of a very ancient, wise woman. For this reason, the plant is affectionately referred to as *ta:g'amih*, "grandmother."[11] When a specimen of *D. stramonium* is harvested, after making an offering of three small pebbles or a pair of short branches, the Indigenous of the region utter a special prayer to the spirit:

> Grandmother, do us a favor and cure the illness [name of person] is suffering from. Here we pay you, we carry [the plant] to see what illness [she or he] has. We are sure that you will remedy [the illness].[12]

The seeds are then eaten in a ceremonial setting for the purpose of divining a proper diagnosis or prognosis of the illness. The Yucatec Maya addressed this sacred herb as *mehen xtoh-k'uh*, the "little plant in the direction of the gods."[13]

Yet a third variety of MIIS pottery—human head effigy pots— was found to contain tropane alkaloids, thus signaling the use of *Datura* spp. in Southeastern ritual activities. We have already seen that the chunkey-related iconography of the Cahokians and other

◎ ◎ ◎

Fig. 7.5. Human head effigy pots.
Photo by the author

Mississippians included the brandishing of severed heads by the game's victors. However, as explained above, those depictions may not have been flesh-and-blood heads at all, but rather these *Datura*-related human head effigy pots. As in pok-ta-pok, the eternal cosmic conflict betwixt the forces of light and those of darkness was ritually played out by the Mississippians in the Southeastern game of chunkey. The supremacy of the power of light or of darkness was quite literally believed to be contingent upon the winners and losers of this ritual game.[14]

In the K'iché Mayan creation epic called *Popol Vuh*, the Hero Twins, Hunahpú and Xbalanqué, avenged the death of their father, the Maize God—whose severed head had come to replace the standard rubber ball—in a grizzly Below World game of pok-ta-pok against the gods of death. The culmination of this story centered upon the recovery of the Maize God's cranium from the powers of darkness and the resurrection of his body. In the mythological charter for the Mississippian

version of the rite, it was the cultural hero Red Horn, who found himself in a life-or-death game of chunkey against the monstrous giants
residing in the Below World. Unable to compete with their skill (which
included trickery), the father of the Hero Twins succumbs, just like in
the Mayan version, to the minions of the Below World, resulting in the
cranium of Red Horn being severed and buried beneath the chunkey
court. The Hero Twins, succeeding in avenging their headless father by
defeating the giant monsters and recovering Red Horn's cranium from
beneath the field—thanks to the mystical powers of Thrown-Away—
succeed in recovering their father's head from beneath the court before
magically reanimating his lifeless corpse. The visually shocking human
head effigy pots recovered in and around the Lower Mississippi Valley
are thus explicitly related to this episode from the Southeastern Hero
Twins myth.[15] Therefore, just like the figures represented by the other
two *Datura*-tainted vessels, the Great Serpent and Earth Mother,
the severed head of the Hero Twins' father is possessed of a distinct
chthonic, Below World significance. *Datura* spp. were inherently tied to
the Below World and its corresponding motifs, while their ceremonial
consumption must have played a significant role in the ritualizations of
particular Underworld charter myths. Perhaps unsurprisingly, human
head effigy pots were also important to certain secretive religious sodalities in the Lower Mississippi Valley.[16]

  Also worth noting in this context is a ceramic white-on-red painted
bottle recovered from one of the final mantle burials in Mound C at
the Moundville site in Alabama, featuring the coiled proboscis and
spotted wings of the *Manduca sexta* moth. In their landmark study,
"Identification of a Moth/Butterfly Supernatural in Mississippian Art,"
anthropologists Vernon James Knight and Judith A. Frank describe this
so-called Nashville Negative Painted bottle.

  The design before us consists of broad, pendant semi-circular elements
  with dotted decoration and a fringed border. The elements alternate
  with pendant, rayed spirals. The whole design, we suggest, is a pars
  pro toto representation of the moth supernatural, in which only the

two most distinctive traits, the dotted, fan-like wings and the feathered proboscis, were deemed sufficient to indicate the whole.[17]

Currently housed at the Gilcrease Museum in Tulsa, Oklahoma, this remarkable artifact, too, tested positive for *Datura*'s tropane alkaloids, according to Eric D. Singleton, curator of ethnology at the National Cowboy and Western Heritage Museum in Oklahoma City.[18]

Conversely, of the eighteen marine shell cups tested by the team of researchers who authored the report cited above, more than three-quarters of the vessels tested positive for *Datura*'s tropane alkaloids. At least one of those displayed an almost caduceus-like lacing of serpents executed in what appears to be the Holly Bluff style, reminiscent of a Celtic knot. We have already seen that such makeshift receptacles were intimately associated with black drink and its ceremony. Previously, marine shell cups were thought to be primarily connected with the consumption of cassina—that is, *Ilex vomitoria* or yaupon holly—but the presence of tropane alkaloids proves Rafferty's hypothesis that certain, often secretive, plants and herbs were added to the ritual libation. As we'll see below, it is highly likely that other plant additives were often included as well.

Another indicator of *Datura* use in the Mississippian Ideological Interactive Sphere is the preoccupation with a very special species of *Lepidoptera*—the above mentioned *Manduca sexta*—known to Natives of South America as the mother of tobacco.[19] Indeed, the tobacco moth, also known as the hawk or sphinx moth—the latter on account of the catlike appearance of the *Manduca sexta* larva when it raises and rears back its head—is the sole pollinator of both *Datura* and *Nicotiana* spp., exclusively laying its eggs upon, eating, and, as a full-grown moth drinking with its lengthy, uncoiled proboscis the nectar of *Datura* and *Nicotiana* spp. We have discussed the association of this Mothra or Mothman with certain shell gorgets executed in the Hightower style, suggesting a shamanic, transformative association with these *Lepidoptera*. Whether pars pro toto or in full, veneration for the tobacco moth is not unique to the MIIS but appears even in Southwestern iconography, depicted on a number of pots and bowls, as petroglyphs, and even scrawled upon the walls of caves—such as California's infamous Pinwheel Cave, located some eighty kilometers northeast of Santa Barbara. There, we find the upper abdomen and head of a *Manduca sexta* painted alongside spiraling delineations of immature *Datura metel* flowers—hence the name Pinwheel Cave. In fact, in 2020, a team of researchers discovered the chewed quids of the leaves of *Datura metel* tucked under various rocks littering the cave floor.[20] The Chumash, who occupied the cave, were also known to give a concoction of *Datura*, called *momoy*, to pubescent boys as young as eight years of age as an essential spiritual rite of passage.[21]

The jagged chevron/zigzag motif on the wings of the sphinx moth is particularly prevalent. Rendered in red ocher, for example, this design decorates a wall in Picture Cave 2.[22] Similar images appear almost 1,845 kilometers away in Dripping Springs, New Mexico, in the form of pictographic rock art left on at least two dozen separate decorated panels. Under each iteration of the jagged, toothy mouth–like motif, researchers found certain notable plants flourishing. "Over a swath of the Chihuahuan Desert stretching from Carlsbad to Las Cruces," the article states,

> at least 24 rock art panels have been found bearing the same distinctive pictographs: repeated series of triangles painted in combinations of red, yellow, and black. And at each of these sites, archaeologists have noticed similarities not just on the rock, but in the ground. Hallucinogenic plants were found growing beneath the triangle designs, including a particularly potent species of wild tobacco and the potentially deadly psychedelic known as datura.

"Researchers believe that the plants may be a kind of living artifact," notes the article announcing this remarkable discovery, "left there nearly a thousand years ago by shamans who smoked the leaves of the plants in preparation for their painting." While the author describes the design as "triangles," the fact of the matter is that they're triangles *executed in rows*. Moreover, every other example appears inverted, with the base of each shape touching, corner to corner, thus producing a variation on the chevron/zigzag motif found in Picture Cave 2.[23] Similarly, while visiting the Deer Valley Petroglyph Reserve in Glendale, Arizona, author and lecturer Jaime Paul Lamb and I found growing underneath virtually every single petroglyph—although they were not examples of variations on this same jagged theme—large specimens of *Nicotiana obtusifolia* and *Datura metel*, from which we collected a number of seeds. "These plants must just grow everywhere out here," Lamb speculated. Under the brutal Arizona sun, we proceeded to walk large portions of the remaining forty-seven acres constituting the reserve, searching for specimens that were not growing below a petroglyph. Strangely, we could not locate a single specimen of either *N. obtusifolia* or *D. metel* growing anywhere else on the reserve except beneath those ancient petroglyphs. Granted, this is a case of Southwestern and not Southeastern Native American culture, but it seems important enough to note while on the subject.

Therianthropic moths also appear in Mesoamerica, decorating a number of Aztec codices and carved in stone, adorning Aztec temples. In *Codex Telleriano-Remensis*, *Codex Rios*, and *Codex Tonalamatl*, for example, the death goddess, Itzpapalotl (Nahuatl), is depicted in the form of a moth. At Tula, moreover, she was shown flying barebreasted and with a death's head. On an altar housed at the Museum of Anthropology in Mexico City, the goddess appears as a fully formed moth having fifteen eyelets spotting the back of her open wings. Finally, an image of Itzpapalotl was left on the keystone of a tomb in Teotenango, Mexico. The Mexican entomologist Carlos Rommel Beutelspacher Baigts penned the following interpretation of this fascinating relic.

Itzpapalotl, drawing taken from the "Keystone of a Tomb, Teotenango, Mexico," was originally identified as a "true vulture with the body and wings of a butterfly," but we are confident that this is Itzpapalotl by the wings, the circles (star signs) that are presented in the wings and thorax, the presence of claws, and of course the head of coscacuauhtli or "true vulture" which show from various sources a close relationship with Itzpapalotl, and according to Beyer, "the buzzard (king vulture) is also the animal of the goddess Itzpapalotl." On the other hand, there was an order of Teotenango Matlalzinca warriors called precisely Coszcacuauhtli.[24]

The presence of circular "star signs"—and especially of claws—is particularly reminiscent of the therianthropic Dances with Mothra shell gorgets recovered from the graves of a number of females at Etowah. Moreover, at the mention of *coscacuauhtli*, or "true vulture," one cannot help but be immediately reminded of the captious Raptor on the Path.

It isn't just the moth that Native Americans were concerned with, however. Even the immature larva of the species—the tobacco hornworm, as it is called, on account of its single, red horn that protrudes from its body—was of great interest to the Mississippians in Moundville, Etowah, and Spiro. And, it's no wonder why. Normally, nicotine is toxic to the majority of insects—hence its use as a potent insecticide. However, this is not true for the tobacco hornworm. Possessed of a specialized protein (CYB6B46) that binds to nicotine and neutralizes the compound, the larvae of *Manduca sexta* are able not only to feed upon the leaves of *Nicotiana* spp., but they're able to retain indefinitely within their bodies the toxin, which they're able to eject at will as a powerful defense mechanism—both "spitting" out the juices in a bluish secretion and exhaling it in the form of a vapor or gas.[25] The same may be true in relation to tropane alkaloids, which the larvae acquire by feeding on its only other host, *Datura* spp. Moreover, insofar as the alkaloids consumed during the insect's larval stage are retained within the bodies of the developing pupae, and finally within the constitutions of the moths themselves—making them a bitter deterrent for any animal unlucky enough to try to eat them—it is possible that the *Manduca sexta* itself is psychoactive.

Fascinatingly, even the intoxicating secretion of the tobacco hornworm was evidently exploited as an inebriant by some Native Americans. For instance, according to Navajo lore, the caterpillars themselves were employed in an entheogenic context. In his book *Navajo Legends*, ethnologist Washington Matthews related the following tale of an Indigenous trial by fire:

> As the boys were about to enter the door they heard a voice whispering in their ears: "St! Look at the ground." They looked down and beheld a spiny caterpillar called Wasekede, who, as they looked, spat out two blue spits on the ground. "Take each of you one of these," said Wind, "and put it in your mouth, but do not swallow it."[26]

Just like with the juice of the tobacco plant, the defensive, nicotine-rich secretions of Wasekede are not to be swallowed but spat out. This would have engendered an ASC much like that offered by the tobacco itself. Immediately following this Wasekede episode, the boys in the story go on to smoke "the tobacco [that] kills"—ostensibly jimsonweed—from a sacred calumet. It is likely that this myth served as a charter for very real rites of passage, not unlike the use of *momoy* among pubescent Chumash.

Images of this tobacco hornworm are preserved in a number of notable Mississippian relics, including a single exquisite crystal caterpillar effigy, delicate as well as intricate,[27] and a stunning shell carving of this significant insect in profile[28]—both recovered from Spiro in Oklahoma. Perhaps the most interesting example appears on the Middle Tennessee Thurston Tablet, found at or near the Castalian Springs Mounds in the late 1800s and currently on display at the Tennessee State Museum. Documenting the various adventures of the Hero Twins, the Thurston Tablet shows the tobacco hornworm being presented in the hands of one of the depicted figures. Paradoxically, this strange creature is associated with deities other than the Hero Twins. On account of his single red horn, the tobacco hornworm may be related not only to the cultural hero known as Red Horn, but also to the malevolent entity, the Great Serpent. Truly, the Algonkian Shawnee, for example, describe this herpetic supernatural as being possessed of "one red horn," while the Northeastern Algonkian Micmac confess that "Abichkam," as he was known, is "no larger than a worm."[29]

The psychological and physiological effects of *Datura* intoxication are considerable. Suffice it to say that *Datura* spp. induce a profound inebriation characterized by dilated pupils, impaired vision, dry mouth, dizziness, headache, and infamously reified visual and aural hallucinations that are next to impossible to distinguish from waking reality. The mnemonic "hot as a hare, blind as a bat, dry as a bone, red as a beet, and mad as a hatter" is a fair description of one who is under the influence of *Datura* spp.[30] Take jimsonweed (*D. stramonium*), for example. Named after a humorous but no doubt frightening episode at Jamestown ("Jamestown weed") during Bacon's Rebellion in 1676, American historian Robert Beverley Jr. recorded in his 1705 book, *The History and Present State of Virginia*:

> The James-Town Weed (which resembles the Thorny Apple of Peru, and I take to be the plant so call'd) is supposed to be one of the greatest coolers in the world. This being an early plant, was gather'd very young for a boil'd salad, by some of the soldiers sent thither to quell the rebellion of Bacon [. . .]; and some of them ate plentifully of it, the effect of which was a very pleasant comedy, for they turned natural fools upon it for several days: one would blow up a feather in the air; another would dart straws at it with much fury; and another, stark naked, was sitting up in a corner like a monkey, grinning and making mows [grimaces] at them; a fourth would fondly kiss and paw his companions, and sneer in their faces with a countenance more antic than any in a Dutch droll. In this frantic condition they were confined, lest they should, in their folly, destroy themselves—though it was observed that all their actions were full of innocence and good nature. Indeed, they were not very cleanly; for they would have wallowed in their own excrements, if they had not been prevented. A thousand such simple tricks they played, and after eleven days returned themselves again, not remembering anything that had passed.[31]

These effects are the result of the interaction of a powerful combination of toxic alkaloids, including scopolamine, hyoscyamine, and atropine. Partial or total amnesia in regard to the incident is also not an uncommon aftereffect. Moreover, this phenomenon was not limited to the Southeast. Indeed, evidence of ceremonial *Datura* deployment spreads well into the region of the Greater Southwest, where there is ample evidence that the use of jimsonweed has persisted for roughly four thousand years.[32]

In addition to *Datura* and tobacco, two other notable nightshades, "known or suspected to have chemical properties capable of inducing mind alterations and even hallucinogenic visions,"[33] were used by the Natives of the Mississippi Valley. Among the analyses of botanical assemblages recovered from various MIIS sites, both black nightshade and morning glory seeds have repeatedly turned up in surprising amounts.[34] Let us first consider black nightshade.

Previously, references to black nightshade use among Southeastern Natives had been the cause of considerable confusion, for there are at least three plants currently found in North America that answer to that same name. However, one of them, *Solanum americanum*—which does not appear to be particularly psychoactive—is predominantly Southwestern in range and was thus largely inaccessible to the Southeastern MIIS. Another, the inebriating *Solanum nigrum*—although now naturalized— is an Old World plant that was introduced to North America with the contact of the Spanish. On the European continent, anthropological archaeologist Casey R. Barrier informs us that,

> nightshade is famous for having been one of the active components of witches' ointments and brews (that would produce realistic dream-states of flight, as well as numerous other hallucinations).[35]

"At low- to mid-range doses," she continues, "this plant causes intense dreams and waking hallucinations [. . .] acting on the brain and nervous system to allow altered [states of consciousness] and dream states to rise to the level of waking consciousness."[36] But still, while *S. nigrum* indeed sounds like a promising lead, it was completely unknown to the Natives of the New World during the precontact era.

The third candidate, on the other hand, known as eastern black nightshade, *Solanum ptycanthum*—a notably potent intoxicant—is possessed of a much wider distribution, covering the majority of the continent east of the Rocky Mountains. Paleobotanist Kathryn E. Parker and ethnobotanist Mary L. Simon explain in their important paper, "Magic Plants and Mississippian Ritual," that "recent refinements in taxonomy [. . .] conclude that *S. ptycanthum* is the correct attribution."[37]

The authors continue,

Biochemical assay has demonstrated the presence of a highly toxic steroidal alkaloid, solanine, in all parts of the eastern black nightshade plant. [. . .] The ingestion of steroidal alkaloids in nightshade causes disruption of cell membranes, especially in the intestines, and may also affect the sympathetic nervous system, resulting in loss of smooth muscle control. Depending on the amount of the alkaloid consumed, symptoms include abdominal pain, nausea, vomiting, diarrhea or constipation, excess salivation, drowsiness, reduced circulatory or respiratory effectiveness, loss of consciousness, and, in high, untreated doses, death. [. . .] Although the side effects of consuming black nightshade are potentially serious, its use in Western medicine as a sedative or painkiller is part of recorded history. [. . .] There are references to nightshade being poisonous and to "ceremonial" uses but without specifying the manner or type of ceremony. [. . .] The manner in which Mississippians used black nightshade cannot presently be determined, but contexts of recovery, including frequent association with tobacco, suggest that the use of the two substances may have been combined. Nightshade leaves or berries may have been dried and added to an *N. rustica* smoking mixture to enhance the narcotic potential. Alternatively, the two may well have functioned in a complementary manner as important elements in ritual practices of acquiring altered states [of consciousness] through both physical purging and cognitive disruption.[38]

Moreover, the remains of certain important species of birds, such as swans, hawks, and falcons, are continually recovered in association with eastern black nightshade and other entheogens. This avian pairing, coupled with the ritual application of *S. ptycanthum*, suggests a clear shamanic connection within the minds of the Natives to the powerful spirits located in the Above World.[39]

Turning our attention now to the other of the two Solanaceae known to the MIIS in addition to *Datura* and tobacco—the equally complicated case of the morning glory vine—it, too, has been the source of no small amount of confusion. By far, *Ipomoea* is the largest genus in the Convolvulaceae family, consisting of some one thousand species—forty-two of which are native to North America. While that narrows our field of investigation down considerably, we're still impeded by the lack of evidence in regard to the effects of some of those native species. However, morning glories have a long history of use in Central America as both a purgative and an entheogen, and it is unlikely that they would have been used much differently by the Indigenous peoples of Southeastern North America.

Veneration for morning glory spp. was so marked that Amerindians of the Formative and Early Caddo periods were wont to depict the vine's characteristic serpentine undulations in intricate, curvilinear, decorative designs, delicately delineated upon the bulging faces of mortuary pots—likely intended, as Reilly suggests, to indicate to their viewers the visionary beverage secreted inside the vessel. Even the unique Caddo-style projectile points—chipped stone arrowheads, most measuring no more than an inch in length, with long, needle-shaped tips, bulbous midsections, pronounced barbs, and prominent basal attachments—which were commonly interred with Caddoan cadavers, were intentionally fashioned to be visually indistinguishable from what may be described as "petrified morning glory leaves."[40] Truly, morning glory spp. appear to have been an essential component of Southeastern Amerindian shamans' psychedelic pharmacopeia.

One species known to Central America that is worth mentioning is *Ipomoea purga*, commonly known in Mexico as jalap and in the United States—particularly among African American "root workers" or practitioners of Hoodoo or "conjure"—as High John the Conqueroo

(Conqueror) root, named after an Afro-American folk hero, comparable to San Simon or Maximón in the Guatemala Highlands. As the name of this species suggests, *Ipomoea purga* is a powerful purgative, and it has been employed toward that end, as far as Britain and India, for centuries. In her fascinating book, *Mojo Workin': The Old African American Hoodoo System*, anthropologist Katrina Hazzard-Donald provides a nice, condensed—yet considerably comprehensive—history of its use.

> Known also as bindweed and as jalap root, its botanical name *Ipomoea jalapa* or *Ipomoea purga* indicates its kinship with the sweet potato, *Ipomoea patata*. It is sometimes classed as convulvolacea jalapa. Its most commonly known name, jalap, is derived from the region in Mexico—Xalapa, Veracruz—where this native plant grows in abundance and from where most of the stock used in Hoodoo has been imported. Jalap's other names include [. . .] *Mechoacan de guerrero* or *Michoacan de guerrero* [and] indicates the Hispanicizing of a Nahuatl Indian name indicating a region with abundant fish. The Spanish term *guerrero* means "warrior." This linguistic combination points to a coastal area where warriors made a reputation, such as the coastal area of Veracruz, Mexico, where Xalapa is the capital city and jalap is said to be native to the area and can grow in abundance there. In fact, this region of Mexico is jalap's only native habitat.
>
> The Xalapa region was inhabited by Teochichimecs, Totonocs, and Nahua-speaking peoples prior to an Aztec or Mexica conquest during the latter half of the fifteenth century. According to Patrick J. Carroll, the Aztecs modified the local economy, demanding greater production of "certain items such as purga de Jalapa, a medicinal herb that grew naturally in the area." When the Spaniards arrived in Mexico in the fifteenth century, they discovered the plant in its native abundance. The roots exported to Europe by the Spaniards in the middle 1500s were collected from the extensive natural populations then growing in the region of Xalapa-Xico in the state of Veracruz. The increased European demand eventually led to commercial cultivation. Between the mid-sixteenth and

early seventeenth centuries, the plant was introduced into various
European botanical gardens in France and England to attempt its
cultivation. The British eventually introduced the species to Jamaica
and India where it is cultivated. The demand for the root continued to increase, and between 1761 and 1851 the Xalapa-Xico region
of Veracruz exported more than one and a half million tons of the
root to Europe, where it was used in treatment of several maladies.
Its most frequent use was as a purgative, laxative, and treatment for
kidney disorders.[41]

As Hazzard-Donald reports, *Ipomoea purga*, similar to a potato, produces a small, tuberous, fusiform rootstock. African American root
workers, however, prize High John the Conqueroo roots for their perceived magical, empowering, and apotropaic qualities rather than for
their cathartic, purgative properties. Traditionally wrapped in red flan-
nel pouches, Conqueroo roots are carried on the person of the prac-
titioner in the form of a gris-gris or mojo bag[42]—a type of amulet or
talisman made popular by a number of Delta and North Mississippi
Hill Country bluesmen, who reference the root and its corresponding
"bag" in their lyrics, although, despite its magical applications, *I. purga*
does not qualify as an entheogenic species of morning glory. *I. corymbosa*, *I. purpurea*, *I. violacea*, *I. pes-caprae*, and *I. leptophylla*, on the other
hand—whose seeds contain powerful visionary compounds—do qual-
ify as entheogens. Additionally, there are at least two other species that
seem promising, albeit questionable, that will require further research
to arrive at any conclusions. These are *I. lacunosa* and *I. hederacea*.

All native to Central America, *I. corymbosa*, *I. purpurea*, *I. violacea*,
I. pes-caprae, and *I. leptophylla* are each known to contain considerable concentrations of the LSD-related visionary alkaloid, ergine,
better known as LSA (d-lysergic acid amide), in their seeds—and in
some cases even in their leaves. Remarkably, these compounds are not
produced by the plant itself but, rather like the kinship of *Claviceps
purpurea* in regard to cereal grains such as rye, wheat, and barley, the
presence of these ergot alkaloids is the result of an ancient symbiotic

relationship between the Clavicipitaceous fungus, *Periglandula*, and its Convolvulaceae host.[43]

The first of these, *I. corymbosa*, also known as Christmas vine, is arguably the most notorious of the four species listed above, as it was famously identified by Richard Evans Schultes, the "father of modern ethnobotany," in 1941 as the mysterious and elusive *ololiuqui* ("that which causes turns") of the Aztecs of north and central Mexico—known to the Mayans in southeastern Mexico as *xtabentún* ("jeweled cord"). Almost two decades later, *Rivea corymbosa*, as it was called at the time, was described in a paper by the "father of LSD," Swiss chemist Albert Hofmann.[44] However, this remarkable entheogenic plant received one of its first descriptions from Francisco Hernández, the physician to the King of Spain, over three centuries prior to 1960. Hernández wrote of it in his seventeenth-century index of Mexican plants and their traditional religious and medicinal applications,

Index medicamentorum, Oliliuhqui, which some call coaxihuitl, or snake-plant, is a twining herb with thin, green, cordate leaves; slender, green, terete stems; and long, white flowers. [. . .] Formerly, when the priests wanted to commune with their gods and to receive a message from them, they ate this plant to induce a delirium. A thousand visions and satanic hallucinations appeared to them.[45]

The sixteenth-century ethnography *The Florentine Codex*, by a priest of the Order of Friars Minor offers a similar etic description. Friar Bernardino de Sahagún writes,

[Ololiuqui] inebriates one; it makes one crazy, stirs one up, makes one mad, makes one possessed. He who eats of it, he who drinks it, sees many things that will make him afraid to a high degree. He is truly terrified of the great snake that he sees for this reason.[46]

A more contemporary report (1960s) was published by neuroscientist Oliver Sacks in his 2012 national bestseller, *Hallucinations*. "About twenty minutes after eating," the author writes, "I felt intense nausea, but when it subsided, I found myself in a realm of paradisiacal stillness and beauty, a realm outside time."[47] Having ingested the seeds on a number of occasions myself, I can personally attest to Sacks's account. The psychedelic effects of ingesting the seeds of certain species of morning glory are attributed specifically to the interference of neuro-receptors that mediate serotonin in humans. This convulsive action of LSA also interferes with dopamine and adrenaline. In addition to nausea and hallucinations, symptoms of ergine intoxication can include tremors, tingling, vertigo, headache, sweating, and uncontrollable muscle movements.[48]

There is some disagreement and confusion regarding two of the above-cited species of morning glory: *I. purpurea* and *I. violacea*. To the Aztecs, *I. purpurea*, the purple morning glory, was known by the name *mecapatli*, meaning "cord medicine."[49] According to German anthropologist Christian Rätsch, *I. purpurea* is probably not entheogenic.[50] However, citing a 1963 analysis of the species that verified the presence of LSA, American psychologist James Fadiman wrote that the "seeds of *Ipomoea purpurea*, the common climbing morning glory, [. . .] have been found to have similar psychedelic properties [to *I. corymbosa*]."[51] Assuming Fadiman is correct, the confirmed abundance of the purple morning glory in Southeastern North America makes it a good candidate for at least one of the species of *Ipomoea* revered and exploited by the Mississippian peoples. As to the question of whether or not *I. purpurea* was introduced to the area by the Spanish colonists, botanists have yet to reach a definitive conclusion.[52]

I. violacea, on the other hand, often confused with *I. corymbosa*, was known to the Aztecs as *tlitliltzin* ("black divine") and to the Zapotecs of Oaxaca as *badoh negro* ("black badoh"). The Mayans knew the *I. violacea*, the violet morning glory, as *xha'il* ("that from the water").[53] The use of *I. violacea*, which is sometimes sold under the name *I. tricolor*, was described by a sixteenth-century monk of the Order of Saint Benedict. In his work, *Breve Relación de los Dioses y Ritos de la Gentilidad*, Dom Pedro Ponce de Leon wrote,

On the ways in which one finds lost objects and other things that
people want to know: They drink [. . .] a seed which they call
tlitlitzin. These are so strong that they sedate the senses and that—
so they say—little black men appear before them which tell them
what they want to know about. Others say that Our Lord appears
to them, while still others that it is angels. And when they do this,
they enter a room, close themselves in, and have someone watch so
that they can hear what they say. And it is not allowed for people
to speak to them before they have reawakened from their delirium,
lest they go insane. And then they ask what they have said, and that
is so.[54]

The Zapotecs would often consume the seeds in pairs, thirteen male
and thirteen female.[55] They consider the black seeds of *ololiuqui* as
macho, "male," while the lighter colored seeds of *tlitliltzin* are thought
of as *hembra*, "female." To the Mixe, who prefer the more powerful
tlitliltzin over *ololiuqui*, the two species are still regarded as "siblings."[56]

I. *leptophylla* and I. *pes-caprae* are also high on the list of poten-
tial candidates. According to recent research, 21 of 21 populations of
I. *leptophylla*, common in the northern Great Plains region, contained
ergine, among other ergot alkaloids, while in 38 of 38 populations of
I. *pes-caprae*, common on the beaches of Florida, LSA was present.[57]
According to Parker and Simon, the morning glory species "unques-
tionably ergine positive that is nearest geographically to the American
Bottom is I. *pes-caprae*, native to the Southeast in coastal areas from
Texas to Georgia."[58] Indeed, it is almost as ubiquitous in the Southeast
as I. *purpurea*.

Finally, although evidence of historical, entheogenic usage is want-
ing, two species of morning glory that are very common in the American
Bottom, I. *lacunosa* and I. *hederacea*, seem quite promising. While they
do not contain ergine specifically, psychoactive and even psychedelic
compounds were found to be present in the two species. Also known
as whitestar, I. *lacunosa*, for instance, produces a potato-like tuber, similar to I. *purga*, that was traditionally consumed by a number of Native

American tribes—including the Chiricahua Apaches. Individual alkaloids identified in the seeds of the species by thin layer chromatography and cochromatography included chanoclavine, elymoclavine, penniclavine, and ergosine—among others.[59] According to Charles I. Abou-Chaar, a past professor of pharmacy at the American University of Beirut, chanoclavine, elymoclavine, and penniclavine are all known to be psychoactive compounds.[60] Moreover, penniclavine and elymoclavine are reported to be psychotropic,[61] while ergosine is one of several alkaloids that the species shares with *Claviceps purpurea*—the infamous ergot fungus.[62] One of the early phytochemical studies on *I. hederacea*, conversely, similarly reported the isolation of the psychoactive alkaloids, chanoclavine, penniclavine, and elymoclavine, with the addition of lysergol—also a psychotropic—from seeds. Perhaps most significantly, the alkaloid isopenniclavine—a reported psychedelic—was also noted.[63]

The presence of all of these compounds in the above-listed species makes them promising candidates for the variety or varieties of morning glories that played such an important role in the MIIS, although, the lack of ergine in some of them rightfully raises warranted questions. In any case, that one or more of these psychoactive or psychedelic species of *Ipomoea* were known to and used by the Mississippians is certain. To discover which one(s) in particular, however, further research is needed.

Setting aside the subject of psychedelic Solanaceae, the penultimate category of entheogens to be here discussed is that of hallucinogenic fungi. While they were well known in Central America, mushrooms are not generally thought of as being connected to the Indigenous cultures of North America. Indeed, among the Wisconsin Ojibwa, for instance, Anishinaabe children, from a very early age, are instructed never to touch four things: "flaming fire, animals with running sores, Grandfather Rattler, and the *Oshtimisk* (Red Top) *Wajashauki* [mushroom]"—that is, *Amanita muscaria*.[64] Such aversions are consistent with "father of ethnomycology" R. Gordon Wasson's theory regarding the presence of pronounced mycophobia among a number of different Western cultures.[65] However, it must be admitted that, oftentimes, such safeguards are due not necessarily to a legitimately perceived inherent danger but instead may be attributable to the ensured maintenance of a healthy relationship and sense of the sacred with regard to the particular taboo object. "Very often," says Rätsch, "the noninitiated populace regards ritual plants and fungi with psychoactive effects (e.g., fly agaric mushrooms, thorn apple, henbane) as poisonous, or at least very dangerous."[66] Of course, in the case of *Amanita muscaria* mushrooms—which can be quite toxic at certain high doses—the prohibition may encompass both reasons.

Ojibwa medicine woman Keewaydinoquay Pakawakuk Peschel, an elder of the Crane clan and initiate of Midéwiwin, once related a story that her instructor in plant matters relevant to the Grand Medicine Society relayed to her regarding *A. muscaria* mushrooms. "If the plants were immature or red," wrote Peschel, "she smashed them." "If they were old and dried," having transitioned from a ruddy vermilion to a mahogany brown, the medicine woman continued, her Midé instructor "gathered them and later burned them in a small stone slab oven." For, according to Peschel's teacher, the old and dried specimens "are the worst of all." The elder of the Crane clan then told the following cautionary tale:

> A wicked sorcerer, a tent shaker [i.e,. a Jessakid], had many wives, sometimes as many as seven at a time. He made a decoction from the *oshtimisk*. "Whatever was in it, it made them leave everything and anyone else and want to be with him. They said they saw colored lights and heard beautiful music and had at last found true happiness."
>
> A young girl who told her that she was in love with the chief's son and wanted some love magic to attract him. The woman refused, so the girl went to the shaman, who "gave her to drink of the *Oshtimiskwabo* and took her in his arms, and behold, he was more handsome than the chief's son . . . Handsome! That rat had yellow teeth, a twisted body, and the eyes of a snake."[67]
>
> He would get them to come to him for some charm or other, and then have them drink this decoction he made from the *Oshtimisk*. . . .
>
> They washed that salamander's slimy clothes, and mended his lodge, and cleaned up his filth, and didn't half know what they were doing . . . .[T]hey lived in a half-world where nothing was real.[68]

While Peschel's story is terrible as it is remarkable, it tells us nothing in regard to the potential shamanic applications of the fungus concerning the Path of Souls. Her account does, however, make it blatantly clear that among the Ojibwa, *A. muscaria* mushrooms were indeed possessed of well-known magical applications that some Jessakid sorcerers apparently had no problem exploiting toward their own selfish ends.

As far as the relation of those "death-dreamers"[69] to the afterlife—and therefore to the Path of Souls—is concerned, American anthropologist Frances Densmore documented the following typical funeral rite performed for initiates by the Midéwiwin.

> Frequently, his face, moccasins, and blanket were painted with brown fungus and vermilion. A round spot of brown was placed on each cheek and over it was painted a horizontal line of vermilion. His moccasins were painted brown, and there were brown streaks on his blanket.
>
> This custom has its origin in the following tradition: It is said that a woman went into a trance for half a day and, on recovering, said that she had been to the ghost land where the northern lights are shining, and that the ghosts held this fungus in their hands and painted their faces in stripes with it. She said that the northern lights are ghosts rising and falling in the steps of a dance, that the women are dressed in gay clothing, and that the warriors have their war clubs. Thus the dead were arrayed to join the dance of the ghosts where the northern lights are shining. [. . .] Rev. J.A. Gilfillan, who witnessed many native burials at White Earth while a missionary among the Indians, quotes an address by an old Indian to the dead body of his daughter, beginning with the words, "Your feet are now on the road of souls . . ."[70]

The "road of souls" is of course our Path of Souls. In the pre-Columbian fly agaric cult of the Americas, *A. muscaria* was known as the underworld mushroom and was thought to put one in contact with the Below World—constituting a sort of doorway leading directly to the domain of the dead.[71] The mention of the northern lights in Densmore's description is immediately reminiscent of Peschel's assertion that women who had drunk *oshtimisk* "saw colored lights"—stated by Densmore's informant to be "ghosts rising and falling in the steps of a dance." In *Chippewa Customs*, a picture accompanies the anthropologist's description that shows an oval-shaped pileus painted on both cheeks of the dead, with a horizontal stipe running from the center of each oval toward the deceased's ears. That the spirits of the dead are said to hold such specimens in their spectral hands is strange as it is compelling. For example, recall the sacred bird-topped poles that are placed along the center of the Midéwigan, representative of the various ascending degrees of the Midéwiwin "Medicine Society." According to Hoffman, one of those posts was curiously rendered red with numerous white spots, reminiscent of the visual appearance of the *A. muscaria* mushroom. At the top of this painted post was precariously placed a stuffed owl—Ko-Ko-Ka-O being the Manitou who guides the dead from the Dzhibai' Midéwigân or Ghost Lodge to the Path of Souls. It is tempting to interpret this rebus as a symbolic surrogate for *A. muscaria*. As author and mycophile Clark Heinrich notes, the fruiting body of *A. muscaria* resembles nothing so much as a bird on a pole.

> When the [*A. muscaria*] mushroom cap begins to invert, the white gills take on the appearance of feathers, and when viewed from the side the cap resembles the outstretched wings of a bird; the dropped annulus takes the part of the bird's tail feathers.[72]

The image of a bird perched upon a pole is among the earliest cave art associated with shamanism. At Lascaux Cave in Montignac, France, a 17,000-year-old image of a vertical post topped with an avian figure appears situated between a defecating bison and a spirit-journeying shaman. The latter, notably, is shown tilted at a 45 degree angle—a position that Goodman specifically associated with the induction of trance.

Moving from the ethnographical and anthropological domains to that of the archaeological, an artifact known as the mushroom effigy wand, a carved wooden portrayal of a fruiting body, was discovered in the state of Ohio by William C. Mills of the Ohio Historical Society. Found in the heart of Mound 7 at Mound City in Ross County, Mills gave the following description of the relic:

> evidently intended to represent the so-called death-cup, or deadly amanita . . . [the remarkable effigy] had been placed upon a large sheet of mica, and over it were heaped the cremated remains comprising the burial. The length of the effigy is 13 ¼ inches. The speci men is made of wood, covered with thin copper.

Similar effigies were also recovered from the Hopewell site. "We found in the Hopewell altars some small mushroom-shaped objects of copper," Moorehead relates, "and several, which were larger and with longer stems, were discovered."[74] According to Romain, the shape and liminal location of the relics suggest that they may be intended to represent the infamous *A. muscaria* mushroom, which "would have facilitated a trip to the otherworld."[75] Notably, *A. muscaria* is a fairly common fungus in the Buckeye State. Indeed, over the course of three decades, in more than half of the forty-two mushroom-hunting forays made by members of the Ohio Mushroom Society, specimens of *A. muscaria* were encountered.[76]

However, in his massive tome, *The Encyclopedia of Psychoactive Plants*, the late, great Christian Rätsch rejected Mills's proposal that the mushroom effigy wand was intended to be an *Amanita* sp., interpreting it instead as a psilocybin-containing *Psilocybe* sp.—and he may not be wrong. First of all, the stipe is far too long. The stipe on the mushroom effigy wand is approximately 40 centimeters in length, whereas the stipe of an *Amanita muscaria* averages 17.5 centimeters. That amounts to less than half the length of the Mound City artifact. The stipe of some *Psilocybe* spp., on the other hand, can easily approach 40 centimeters. Secondly, the pileus is simply too small. The pileus of the mushroom effigy wand measures 6.35 centimeters in diameter. The average diameter of an *Amanita muscaria* is 14 centimeters. The pileus of some *Psilocybe* spp., conversely, can range from 1.6–8 centimeters in diameter.

In terms of identification, the copper coating of the mushroom effigy wand is of little assistance. For Romain, the "reddish-yellow color of the copper used to cover the wood" is a good indication that *A. muscaria* is intended.[77] And, indeed, *A. muscaria* can take on a distinct brassy, metallic sheen—especially upon drying. However, many *Psilocybe* spp. acquire a burnished, copper-like appearance as well. But, psilocybin-containing mushrooms are notorious for their tendency to stain blue upon handling. In fact, this cerulean characteristic is one of the primary identifying features for fungus foragers. Bruising triggers a distinctive chemical reaction in the fruiting body, making its identification as a psilocybin-containing species possible. Through oxidization and the action of a special pair of unique enzymes, the flesh of the mushroom turns a striking greenish blue if it is broken or bruised. Similarly, via the same chemical process of oxidization, copper oxide, as it collides with carbon dioxide, produces a beautiful blue-green patina effect—that is, the mushroom effigy wand "bruises," not unlike a psilocybin-containing mushroom. Ergo, it is possible to argue for both cases using the copper coating as potential evidence.

Complicating matters even further, in the state of Ohio no less than a dozen psilocybin-containing species are found. These include: *Gymnopilus aeruginosus*, *Gymnopilus luteofolius*, *Gymnopilus luteus*, *Gymnopilus spectabilis*, *Inocybe insignis*, *Panaeolus bisporus*, *Panaeolus cinctulus*, *Pluteus albostipitatus*, *Pluteus americanus*, *Pluteus saupei*, *Psilocybe caerulipes*, and *Psilocybe ovoideocystidiata*. Just judging by the appearance of the wand and the location of its discovery, the last of those listed, *Psilocybe ovoideocystidiata*—the dimensions of which most closely resemble those of the mushroom effigy wand—would seem to be an especially promising candidate. Furthermore, three additional effigies, this time of pilei alone—one hollow and composed of copper, the other two solid, with one carved from milky quartz and the other from limestone—with acute umbones and independent of their stipes, were recovered from the Great Cache in Ohio's Tremper Mound. These also seem to replicate the pileus of *P. ovoideocystidiata*.

A second mushroom effigy—in this case made from solid stone—was recovered from a mound in Fort Ancient, also located in Ohio.

Compared to the Mound City mushroom effigy wand, however, this artifact is rather short and squat, with its stipe rendered in almost the same dimensions as its pileus—the latter being only slightly broader than the former. Visually, it is quite unremarkable. Were it left sitting out on a desk, for instance, one might easily mistake it for a common paperweight. In the estimation of the author, judging solely by the appearance and location, the Fort Ancient artifact most closely resembles an immature specimen of a *Gymnopilus* sp.—most likely, *Gymnopilus luteus* or *Gymnopilus spectabilis*, both of which are known to contain psilocybin. In any case, whether *Amanita* or *Psilocybe*, these Middle Woodland Hopewell mushroom effigies are quite clearly related to the afterlife journey. To quote Romain, who summed up the situation succinctly,

From its liminal location in a burial mound and its association with the dead, it seems likely that the mushroom was important for its mind-altering capabilities. Irrespective of whether the mushroom effigy represents a helper used to facilitate hallucinogenic journeys or to cause death, it is reasonable to think that for the Hopewell, the mushroom provided access to the Otherworld—one way or another.[78]

EIGHT

THE *MISSIHUASCA* HYPOTHESIS

The final entheogenic substance that I'd like to discuss here is considerably more complicated than any of the others that we have thus far covered. For the most part, all of the hypotheses proposed about the hallucinogens presented up to this point have been backed by strong anthropological and archaeological evidence. The following, however, constitutes a purely speculative conjecture that is based largely on ethnographical information. I refer to it tentatively as "the *Missihuasca* hypothesis."

We have seen how many Native American myths became charters for ritual activities, some of which would have served as rites of passage into various stages of Indigenous life. One such myth is preserved in James Mooney's *Myths of the Cherokee*, originally published in 1902 as part of the *Nineteenth Annual Report of the Bureau of American Ethnology*. In one of the myths, titled "Ûñtsaiyĭ', The Gambler," Mooney documents the following trial:

> Thunder lives in the west, or a little to the south of west, near the place where the sun goes down behind the water. In the old times he sometimes made a journey to the east, and once after he had come back from one of these journeys a child was born in the east who, the people said, was his son . . . [Soon] the news came to Thunder

138

⊚ ⊚ ⊚

Fig. 8.1. Thorns of the honey locust tree (*Gleditsia triacanthos*),
which are referenced in Cherokee mythology.
Photo by the author

that a boy was looking for him who claimed to be his son. Said
Thunder, "I have traveled in many lands and have many children.
Bring him here and we shall soon know." So they brought in the
boy, and Thunder showed him a seat and told him to sit down.
Under the blanket on the seat were long, sharp thorns of the honey
locust, with the points all sticking up, but when the boy sat down
they did not hurt him, and then Thunder knew that it was his son.[1]

Known to the Cherokee as *kulsetsi*, honey locust (*Gleditsia triacanthos*,
syn. *Acacia americana*) is a tree possessed of pinnate leaves and dense
clusters of large, sharp thorns—sometimes as much as twenty-five to
thirty centimeters long. The tree was especially important in regard to

gatayûstĭ, the Cherokee ballgame (similar to chunkey), before which the players would chew the honey locust's roots—spitting out the juice, rubbing the spittle all over their bodies. The athletes would also paint crosses atop their hearts and shoulders with a pigment prepared from honey locust trees that had been stuck by lightning *"but not killed."*[2] For, according to the Cherokee, honey locust is said to be sacred to Thunder-man,[3] a notably powerful supernatural entity. *G. triacanthos* is therefore revered as a very sacred tree. We can glean some idea of the degree to which the honey locust was venerated in the following excerpt from the same Gambler myth. In it, the consort of Thunder-man informs the boy that the supernatural arboreal figure,

will send for his other sons to play ball against you. There is a honey-locust tree in front of the house, and as soon as you begin

◉ ◉ ◉

Fig. 8.2. Honey locust (*Gleditsia triacanthos*).

Photo by the author

to get tired strike [your lightning] at that and your father will stop the play, because he does not want to lose the tree. [. . .] At last he was tired from defending himself alone against two, and pretended to aim a blow at the honey-locust tree. Then his father stopped the fight, because he was afraid the lightning would split the tree, and he saw that the boy was brave and strong.[4]

As the Gambler myth makes clear, the boy in the story—perhaps one of the Hero Twins—is associated with lightning.

According to a note included with a North American herbarium specimen of the honey locust tree, "a mead is [. . .] simmered from [the pith of the seed pods]."[5] However, unbeknownst to many anthropologists and botanists, *Gleditsia triacanthos* conceals a visionary secret within the bark of its roots—one that is among the most potent hallucinogenic substances known to humans: *N,N*-dimethyltryptamine. *N,N*-DMT constitutes the active component of a number of South American psychedelic preparations, including *yopo*—a hallucinogenic snuff made from the seeds of *Anadenanthera peregrina*; *nyakwána*—an entheogenic snuff concocted from the resin of *Virola elongata*; and *ayahuasca* or *yagé*—a psychedelic tea prepared from the leaves of *Psychotria viridis* or *Diplopterys cabrerana* in conjunction with the woody vines of *Banisteriopsis caapi*.

That the visionary nature of *G. triacanthos* has gone unnoticed by scholars is understandable. To my knowledge, honey locust's psychoactivity has been noted in but a single published source—and it is one that does not necessarily qualify as academic. In November 1998, a man calling himself Keeper of the Trout published a legendary catalog of various flora known to contain tryptamine alkaloids, titled *Tryptamines from Higher Plants*. Four years later, in April 2002, Trout added tryptamine-containing fungi and fauna to the list, republishing the work as *Some Simple Tryptamines*, which entered its second edition in December 2006—with minor revisions added in May 2007. Raising a single sapling from a *G. triacanthos* seed, a colleague of Trout, known simply as Appleseed, using xanthydrol as a colorimetric reagent, assayed the specimen via thin layer chromatography, finding that *N,N*-DMT was indeed present in the roots of honey locust.

The Pancarú Indians of the eastern Amazon, as well as the Kariri, Tusha, and Fulnio, would employ the *N,N*-DMT-rich roots of *Mimosa hostilis* (syn. *Acacia tenuiflora*), a close cousin of *G. triacanthos*, in the preparation of *jurema preta* drinks, called *ajucá* or *veuêka*—known to induce shamanic states of consciousness that brought on "an enchantment, transporting them to heaven." According to one trusted source,

> An old master of ceremonies, wielding a dance rattle decorated with a feather mosaic, would serve a bowlful of the infusion made from jurema roots to all celebrants, who would then see glorious visions of the spirit land, with flowers and birds. They might catch a glimpse of the clashing rocks that destroy souls of the dead journeying to their goal or see the Thunderbird shooting lightning from a huge tuft on his head and producing claps of thunder by running about.[6]

It is challenging to resist the temptation to read in this description a South American variation of the Path of Souls theme, with the formidable and threatening Raptor on the Path appearing at the culmination of the trip. For the Tukano, correlations to the Path of Souls model are even more explicit.

> [The] shaman's body lies as if dead while his consciousness has taken off into another reality. The shamanic soul has transformed itself into a jaguar and now flies over a rainbow to the Milky Way. The most fantastic colors and forms unfold before the shaman's inner eye. Honeycomb patterns dance by and change into crystals filled with an otherworldly light. Wavy lines flow out and back together into colorful swirls. The jaguar shaman is irresistibly sucked in. The swirls open into a tunnel made of circling skulls, at the end of which shines a warm, blue light. The jaguar shaman has reached the Milky

Way, where he meets the ayahuasca woman who revealed the true reality to humans at the dawn of creation and gave them the secret of the "drink of true reality."[7]

There is one other genus known to and used by the Natives of the Southeast—*Desmanthus illinoensis* (Illinois bundleflower) and *Desmanthus leptolobus* (prairie bundleflower), the former being common from the Midwest to the South of the United States and the latter found more within the vicinity of Picture Cave—that is at least worth mentioning. While the roots do contain considerable amounts of *N,N*-DMT, there is at present no evidence that anything other than the leaves and seeds of these species found use among the Natives of the MIIS.

It is important to note that *N,N*-DMT is not normally orally active in humans on account of the presence of a digestive enzyme, called monoamine oxidase (MAO), under which the tryptamine alkaloid is broken down. But, when β-carboline alkaloids, such as harmine, harmane, norharman, and others—which constitute various types of monoamine oxidase inhibitors (MAOI)—are coadministered, *N,N*,-DMT is rendered pharmacologically active.[8] Without the presence of β-carboline alkaloids, it is unknown whether or not *N,N*-DMT is absorbable by oral mucosa. Ergo, simply chewing the roots of *G. triacanthos* may not elicit any psychedelic response. However, there is evidence in the literature that *N,N*-DMT may be absorbable via transdermal inoculation.[9] Assuming this to be true, it stands to reason that chewing the roots, with the addition of spitting and rubbing the juices upon the skin, may in fact be an effective mode of application. Even so, there are a number of plants that were familiar to and exploited by the Mississippian Ideological Interaction Sphere that are known carriers of various β-carboline alkaloids—including *Nicotiana rustica*, *Passiflora incarnata*, and possibly even *Ilex vomitoria*, all of which were discovered in various botanical assemblages recovered from a number of MIIS sites.[10]

N. rustica was found to contain unknown amounts of

the β-carboline alkaloids harmane and norharman.[11] The tricyclic β-carboline alkaloid harmine is present in considerable amounts in *P. incarnata*—as well as in the South American variety, *P. edulis*.[12] Lastly, the South American yaupon, *Ilex paraguayensis*, better known by its common name, yerba-maté—a close cousin of North America's *Ilex vomitoria*—is possessed of trace amounts of β-carboline alkaloids. If the same is true also of *Ilex vomitoria*, considering the substantial reductions to which cassina was regularly boiled down to create the syrupy black drink, Natives may have been able to arrive at a brew concentrated enough to potentiate *N,N*-DMT. In any case, a U.S. patent filed in 2005 (US6929811B2) relies on an extract of yerba-maté for the specific purpose of modulating MAO activity.[13] Recall that Rafferty noted the addition of certain—perhaps unknown—substances to black drink mixtures. If *N. rustica*, *P. incarnata*, and especially *G. triacanthos* were among those additives, the purgative action of cassina, which by itself does not appear to be an emetic, would be validated. Indeed, the purgative potential of ayahuasca is so pronounced that, in some regions, the brew is known as *la purga*, "the purge."[14] Were any of these plants to be added to *G. triacanthos*, moreover, a potion virtually indistinguishable from ayahuasca, the South American tea, would be the result. Notably, the Cherokee Gambler myth recounted by Mooney does contain evidence that the roots of honey locust were at times "boiled"—and done so in a context directly connected to a threatening ordeal, which likely served as a charter for a legitimate Indigenous rite of passage.

> There was a large pot in the corner and he told his wife to fill it with water and put it over the fire. When it was boiling, he put in some [of the honey locust] roots, then took the boy and put him in with them. He let it boil a long time until one would have thought that the flesh was boiled from the poor boy's bones . . .[15]

While the boy's entry into the pot probably would have amounted to little more than a ceremonial test of courage, the inclusion of the motif

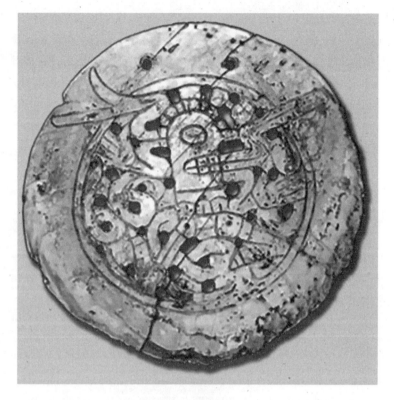

⊙ ⊙ ⊙

Fig. 8.3. A "Spaghetti style" gorget, carved from shell, depicting a
figure submerged in a boiling pot, surrounded by twisting objects
reminiscent of roots. See also color plate 16.

Photo by Herb Roe

of boiling *G. triacanthos* roots is highly suggestive and too compelling
to simply dismiss. And, in fact, a number of extant Spaghetti-style gorgets do appear to depict a human figure submerged in a cauldron, surrounded by twisting, boiling *G. triacanthos* roots.[16] It is this product
that I have proposed to call *Missihuasca*.

Finally, it is essential that among the South American *payés* or
shamans of the Tukano, the consumption of ayahuasca is specifically
associated with the ascent of the spirit to the galactic Path of Souls.
According to the Austrian anthropologist Gerardo Reichel-Dolmatoff,
when the Tukano consume yagé, the payés,

feel they are ascending to the Milky Way. [. . .] The ascent to the
Milky Way is not easily accomplished. An apprentice will hardly
ever be able to rise immediately to this [. . .] region but rather will
learn to do so after many trials. At first he will barely rise over the
horizon, the next time perhaps he will reach a point corresponding
to the position of the sun at 9 a.m., then at 10 a.m., and so on until
at last, in a single, soaring flight, he will reach the zenith.[17]

Reichel-Dolmatoff, who spent a lot of time with the Tukano payés,
explains:

It is said that the individual "dies" when he drinks the potion and
that now his spirit returns to the uterine regions of the Beyond, only
to be reborn there and to return to his ordinary existence when the
trance is over. This then is conceived as an acceleration of time, an
anticipation of death and rebirth.[18]

If my reading of the Cherokee Gambler myth is anywhere close to correct, it would not be improbable that the Natives of the Mississippian
Ideological Interaction Sphere may have employed *Gleditsia triacanthos*,
along with *Nicotiana rustica*, *Passiflora incarnata*, and/or *Ilex vomitoria*,
toward similar—if not identical—anabatic ends.

I have yet to visit a Mississippian site where I did not find honey
locust trees growing directly on or around the mound complexes. This
is not a coincidence. A 2016 study published by American biologist
Robert J. Warren II confirmed that the unnaturally wide distribution of
Gleditsia triacanthos in the Southeastern United States is a direct result
of deliberate human intervention, that the Mississippians—especially
the Cherokee—were intentionally cultivating honey locust trees in and
around their complexes, planting them in numbers that far exceed the
tree's ordinary dispersal.[19] Insofar as *G. triacanthos* is a notoriously hard
and dense wood that is extremely resistant to manipulation—especially
when worked by hand—employing it in anything save extremely small
contexts (such as sticks for *gatayûstĭ*, the Cherokee ballgame) would

have been simply unpractical. And that is to say nothing of the formidable, icepick-like clusters of footlong thorns that cover their trunk and branches, which would have served as a convincing deterrent. It may be the case that honey locust trees were propagated primarily for the use of their thornless roots in preparing the hypothetical Southeastern ayahuasca analogue *Missihuasca*.

CLOSING REMARKS

The Path of Souls is an ancient Amerindian model of the afterlife journey, to which a number of tribes among the Mississippian Ideological Interaction Sphere (MIIS) ascribed a belief. This journey constituted fearsome trials and formidable obstacles that threatened the free-soul of the deceased throughout the duration of the ordeal. The successful completion of these tribulations and subsequent entry into the Land of the Dead were naturally considered grand accomplishments, denoting high honor and considerable courage in the victor. Knowledge of the Path of Souls therefore came to constitute secret, initiatory wisdom, reserved exclusively for the worthy elite—on whose behalf individuals not initiated into the mysteries of the Path of Souls were forced to rely. For the preservation and perpetuation of these hidden mysteries, certain secretive sodalities were organized, structured largely upon the Midéwiwin or Grand Medicine Society, who recorded their secrets by grades or degrees upon the sacred medium of birch-bark scrolls—known to the Ojibwa as *wiigwaasabakoon*. Many of these *wiigwaasa-bakoon* depict the Path of Souls schemata in the form of a ritualized initiation, which aimed to put a candidate *nominally* through the Path of Souls trials that *actually* awaited the initiated upon their physical demise. To aid in these virtual re-creations of the afterlife journey, a number of powerful entheogenic plants, including *Nicotiana rustica*, *Datura* spp., and *Ipomoea* spp., eastern black nightshade, "magic" mushrooms, and perhaps even *Missihuasca*—a Mississippian analogue to the

South American jungle brew, ayahuasca—were employed for the express purpose of inducing profound altered states of consciousness. These shamanic conditions included what we might call near-death experiences or out-of-body experiences and were ritually designed to place a candidate face to face, one degree at a time, with the obstacles that await the free-soul along the Path of Souls. Different substances elicited different encounters, and with each passing experience, the candidate was awarded certain badges of recognition—such as carved marine shell cups and gorgets—that communicated his place within the social hierarchy. The role of entheogenic plant substances among the MIIS therefore cannot be overstated. To be sure, they occupied a frankly central, sacred position in the various complex cosmologies of the Native American peoples residing in the Southeast—and that is true both in regard to their lives and in their deaths.

THE LEGEND OF MISKWEDO

By Keewaydinoquay Pakawakuk Peschel

Attention, I will tell you a story, a story of The People, a story of Miskwedo, that red-topped mushroom which is the spiritual child of Nokomis Giishik, Grandmother Cedar, and of Nimishomiss Wigwass, our Grandfather Birch. Listen and learn.

Certainly this is true, for it was told by our honored forefathers. Now this happened in the long, long ago times, many unaccountable moons gone by and many uncountable trails back, it is thought, at one of the temporary camps during the Great Migration of our people across the continent of Minissah, from the Land of the Sun-rising toward the Land of the Sun-setting, when they were being led by the Divine Megis to our home, to the promised land of Keewaydinaukee.

There were two brothers, so young that they had not yet received their adult names; full brothers they were, both sons of the same woman of the Owl clan and of the same man of the Sturgeon clan. The first born was called Elder Brother and the second born was called Younger Brother. They lived alone together (Oh, Wah-ey-eah) for their parents

---

This essay was published as "The Legend of Miskwedo" in the *Journal of Psychedelic Drugs* 11 (1–2): 1979, 29–31. It is published by permission of Taylor and Francis.

had died bravely along that Great Migration trail. Oh, Wah-ey-eah! They hunted the same quarry, ate the same food, and shared all things in peace and harmony—and that was good. Ahauw!

Now one day, at the place about which this story is told, the boys were very hungry, their stomachs empty. Since there were mountains in that place, they climbed up the rocky slopes looking for food. At last they came to a great cave high in the mountainside. It seemed to them that light came out of the cave opening. An amazing sound, a sound like the humming of uncountable bees, was heard. Very carefully and very quietly the brothers approached, curiously peering through the opening. They saw a beautiful meadow in which there grew many tall red and white mushrooms—handsome wajashkwedeg they were— turning and revolving, buzzing and murmuring, singing a strange song of happiness under a brilliantly sunny sky.

Quick as a flash of lightning, Younger Brother scrambled through the opening, running with joyous abandon into the meadow of murmuring mushrooms.

"Stop! Wait! Stop!" called Elder Brother. "We do not know what Spirits there are in this place. We do not know what they may be."

But Younger Brother did not stop. He was, in fact, already gone!

Younger Brother ran to the tallest, strongest, reddest, most handsome mushroom of them all. White fluffs, like tuft feathers of the finest warbonnet, waved across its shining cap. Streamers of filmy white, like frills of clouds, swirled in rhythm as it revolved. Elder Brother watched aghast as Younger Brother became fused to that giant mushroom's stipe. He beheld Younger Brother begin to grow a bright cap. At first slowly, then faster and faster, Younger Brother began to spin in the sun. Elder Brother was horrified. Quickly he noted the location of the giant mushroom and the position of the little mushroom which had once been his Younger Brother. Then he ran. He ran as fast as his legs would carry him, away from the bewitching meadow, away from the great cave, away from that awful hole in the mountainside. Back down the winding trails, back down the rocky slopes, he ran, never pausing until at last he came to the village.

"Awoohee!"

He gave the emergency call for the elders and the medicine people. Quickly he told them everything that had happened.

"What shall I do?" he begged. "Tell me, Wise Ones, how to save my little brother."

The elders and the medicine people looked at each other. They shook their heads.

"We have never heard of such a thing," they said. "We must ask the Drum."

When they had consulted the Drum, which was a Medicine Drum, they said, "We have an answer, but it is a difficult one. This is what you must do. You must remember every word. You must go to that place called 'The-Place-of-the-Magic-Sands.' It is a high cliff along the lake with a talus slope and great waves pounding the rocks into the sand. There you should collect the magic sands, Onoman. Put them in a deer-skin bag with sacred tobacco and pull the drawstring tightly. Think a prayer of thanksgiving to the Spirits of that place for their making of Onoman (the magic sands). Continue running along the trail until you come to 'The-Place-Where-the-High-Trees-Grow-and-the-Eagles-Nest.' Find the highest tree and the nest of the largest eagle. He is a Thunderbird. You must obtain four feathers from his tail. Think to the Thunderbird a prayer of thanksgiving and petition as you keep on running toward the mountain. Follow the same trail to where the light of the great cave shimmers through the opening in the side of the mountain.

"Now face the East with the eagle feathers in your hand, asking Gitchi Manitou's blessing onto them. Observe which mushroom is the tallest, strongest and the handsomest. He is the chief. With utmost speed enter the witching meadow, thrust an eagle feather through the stipe of the chief. He will stop turning. Now locate the wisest Miskwedo among them, the eldest mushroom who is sprouting, the one with the most influence. As fast as you can, put an eagle feather through the stipe of this mushroom. He, too, will stop turning. Now the third eagle feather must be thrust through the stipe of the mushroom which you know to be Younger Brother. Then dump the bag of magic Onoman all over him. Carefully remove every bit of this mushroom, from the shining cap to the bulb at the foot. Do not break off any particle or part of the Younger Brother will be broken too. Carrying the mushroom with you, hurry through the opening in the mountain. Stop just long enough to place the last protective eagle feather across the opening of the cave, then continue down along the trail as fast as you can go. This is what you are supposed to do.

"As you run away from that mountain, the load (your 'Brother' mushroom) will become heavier and heavier, until finally, it will become as it was in the past. But though you recognize him as being there, as he once was, do not speak, do not stop! As you run, it will become more and more as it was in the past, except for one thing—an eagle feather will protrude from Younger Brother's skin. There it must always remain."

All these things occurred then. They happened as it was foretold they would happen. Elder Brother remembered clearly every little thing. He did exactly as he was told, collecting the magic sands and the eagle feathers. He went through the hole in the side of the mountain, placing the protective eagle feathers and dumping the magic sands over Younger Brother. He rescued Younger Brother, who seemed to become as he was in the past—except for one weird thing: an eagle feather stuck out strangely from his skin just as if it had grown there!

Together the boys ran swiftly down the trail, back to the camp of The People. There they lived once again, in the same lodge, in peace and harmony. And that was good. Ahauw!

Many days and many nights went by. Slowly matters began to change. Wah-ay-eah. Elder Brother arose in the mornings, his heart heavy with sadness and foreboding. He worried and he worried and he was unhappy. Wah-ay-eah. Younger Brother, on the contrary, arose smiling each day, his heart filled with happiness, his lips singing merriment. Ahauw, Zahwendahmowin!

Now Elder Brother noticed that Younger Brother went very frequently behind the wigwam to urinate. He stayed much longer than seemed to be necessary, and particularly, at the full of the moon, he stayed a long, long time. At last Elder Brother, who disliked playing the spy, decided that for his brother's welfare he simply must investigate. So he went out behind the wigwam and discovered, just as he had thought, Little Brother was not urinating. He had already gone down the trail further into the woods. Elder Brother followed secretly until he came to a clearing.

What does he behold? There he sees Younger Brother standing in the center of an open space, a large group of people around him. Younger Brother's arms are open wide, spread like the umbrella of a mushroom. His robes are beautiful, glowing red, and tufts of white feathers adorn his head. In a high, humming voice of happiness, like the song of uncountable bees, he sings to The People.

"Because of my supernatural experience,
In the Land of the Miskwedo
I have a cure to alleviate your ills,
To take away your unhappiness.
If only you will come to my penis
And take the quickening waters flowing from it
You, too, can be forever happy."

Every time the clouds darken the moon, he urinates. The people catch his urine in mokukeg, birch bark containers. They drink this liquid that has been given to them as a great boon by the Miskwedo spirits. All the members of the mushroom cult, all the devotees of Miskwedo, Younger Brother, who is the chief mushroom, the drum chief, the three elders and three sets of lesser officers, come up in turn and sing their Miskwedo song. Throughout the fullness of time these people sing their happy songs, their hearts are strong, and each one does the work of ten.

Wah-ay-eah, poor Elder Brother! He did not understand the ways of the red-topped mushroom. He did not understand the use of the golden mushroom liquid and the penis elixir. He continued to be filled with foreboding.

"Nothing good can come of it," he lamented. He troubled, he worried, and he was unhappy. Oh Wah-ay-eah.

Neither did Younger Brother understand the workings of the Sacred Mushroom. But he went on being happy, and all the people following him continued in a state full of bliss.

And so it is and so it continues to this very day, now at this place and at this time, as it was then, and shall be in the future. All the people who are OLDER BROTHERS, like Elder Brother in our story, because they do not understand, they are unhappy. They trouble, they worry, and they fuss. Neither do the YOUNGER BROTHERS of this world understand, yet they still drink the golden mushroom waters and are happy. They drink the Elixir of the Great Miskwedo, and much is revealed of the supernatural and other knowledge in this way. It is the Kesuwabo—the liquid Power of the Sun—Kesuwabo. Ahauw! Jahwendamowining, ahauw!

NOTES

INTRODUCTION. MEET THE MIIS-SISSIPPIANS

1. Reilly and Garber, "Introduction," in *Ancient Objects and Sacred Realms*, eds. Reilly and Garber, 1–7.
2. Reilly and Garber, "Introduction," in *Ancient Objects and Sacred Realms*, eds. Reilly and Garber, 1–7.
3. Lankford, "The 'Path of Souls': Some Death Imagery in the Southeastern Ceremonial Complex," in *Ancient Objects*, eds. Reilly and Garber, 174–212.
4. Lankford, *Reachable Stars*, 204.
5. Reilly, "The Great Serpent in the Lower Mississippi Valley," in *Visualizing the Sacred*, eds. Lankford, Reilly, and Garber, 118–134.
6. Reilly, "Foundational and Cosmological Themes in Braden-Style Art," in *Recovering Ancient Spiro*, eds. Singleton and Reilly, 220–233.
7. Reilly, "The Great Serpent in the Lower Mississippi Valley," in *Visualizing the Sacred*, eds. Lankford, Reilly, and Garber, 118–134.
8. Lankford, *Native American Legends of the Southeast*, 87.
9. Lankford, *Native American Legends of the Southeast*, 248.
10. Landes, *Ojibwa Religion*, 50–52; Lankford, "Was There a Moundville Medicine Society?" in *Rethinking Moundville*, eds. Steponaitis and Scarry, 74–98.
11. Freidel, Schele, and Parker, *Maya Cosmos*, 276.
12. Lankford, "Local Eyes," in *New Methods and Theories*, eds. Giles and Lambert, 111–130.
13. Benton-Banai, *The Mishomis Book*, 4.

14. Carr, *Being Scioto Hopewell*, 317.

15. Lankford, "Was There a Moundville Medicine Society?" in *Rethinking Moundville*, eds. Steponaitis and Scarry, 74–98.

16. VanPool, "The Shaman-Priests," 696–717.

17. Hoffman, *The Midē'wiwin*, 166–167.

18. Pomedli, *Living with Animals*, 92.

19. Pomedli, *Living with Animals*, 130.

20. Howey and O'Shea, "Bear's Journey."

21. Romain, *Shamans of the Lost World*, 181.

22. Parker and Simon, "Magic Plants and Mississippian Ritual," in *Archaeology and Ancient Religion*, eds. Koldehoff and Pauketat, 117–166; Barrier, "Psychotropic Plants and Sacred Animals at the Washausen Mound-Town," in *Shaman, Priest, Practice, Belief*, eds. Carmody and Barrier, 147–165.

1. NATIVE AMERICAN INTOXICANTS

1. Lankford, *Native American Legends*, 143–144.

2. VanPool and VanPool, *Signs of the Casas Grandes Shamans*, 68.

3. VanPool and VanPool, *Signs of the Casas Grandes Shamans*, 68.

4. VanPool and VanPool, *Signs of the Casas Grandes Shamans*, 66–67; VanPool, "The Shaman-Priests," 696–717.

5. Schultes, Hofmann, and Rätsch, *Plants of the Gods*, 179.

6. Keck, "The Altered States of America."

7. Jay, *Mescaline*, 72–73.

8. Jay, *Mescaline*, 65.

9. Jay, *Mescaline*, 42–43.

10. Myerhoff, *Peyote Hunt*, 221.

11. Myerhoff, "Return to Wirikuta," in *Symposium of the Whole*, eds. Rothenberg and Rothenberg, 225–230.

12. Jay, *Mescaline*, 54.

13. Rätsch, *The Encyclopedia of Psychoactive Plants*, 479–481.

14. Schultes, Hofmann, and Rätsch, *Plants of the Gods*, 57.

15. Lanaud et al., "Revisted History of Cacao Domestication."

16. Thomas H. Maugh II, "Earlier Traces of Cacao Use Found in Southwest," *Los Angeles Times*, February 3, 2009.

17. Rätsch, *The Encyclopedia of Psychoactive Plants*, 501.

18. Lane, *Sacred Mushroom Rituals*, 16.

19. Rätsch, *The Encyclopedia of Psychoactive Plants*, 502.

20. Mowry and Dean, "Analysis of Modern and Ancient Artifacts."

21. Frank, Moore, and Ames, "Historical and Cultural Roots," 344–351.

22. Abbott, "American Indian and Alaska Native Aboriginal Use of Alcohol," 1–13.

23. Tamara, "Ceramic Analysis," 10.

24. Cherrington, "Aborigines of North America," in *Standard Encyclopedia of the Alcohol Problem*, vol. I, ed. Cherrington, 3–42.

25. Mancall, *Deadly Medicine*, 74–75.

26. Trenk, "Religious Uses of Alcohol," 73–86.

27. Szalavitz, "No, Native Americans Aren't Genetically More Susceptible to Alcoholism," *The Verge*, October 2, 2015.

28. Trenk, "Religious Uses of Alcohol," 73–86.

29. Trenk, "Religious Uses of Alcohol," 73–86.

2. A CAVERN OF SACRED VISIONS

1. National Park Service, "Solution Caves."

2. National Park Service, "Prehistoric Cave Discoveries."

3. Simek and Cressler, "Caves as Mortuary Contexts," in *Mississippian Mortuary Practices*, eds. Sullivan and Mainfort Jr., 270–292.

4. Simek and Cressler, "Caves as Mortuary Contexts," in *Mississippian Mortuary Practices*, eds. Sullivan and Mainfort Jr., 270–292.

5. Simek and Cressler, "Caves as Mortuary Contexts," in *Mississippian Mortuary Practices*, eds. Sullivan and Mainfort Jr., 270–292.

6. Bacon et al., "An Upper Palaeolithic Proto-writing System."

7. Simek and Cressler, "Caves as Mortuary Contexts," in *Mississippian Mortuary Practices*, eds. Sullivan and Mainfort Jr., 270–292.

8. Simek and Cressler, "Caves as Mortuary Contexts," in *Mississippian Mortuary Practices*, eds. Sullivan and Mainfort Jr., 270–292.

9. Reilly, "The Cave and the Beneath World Spirit," in *Picture Cave*, eds. Diaz-Granados, Duncan, and Reilly, 133–143.

10. Conway, "The Conjurer's Lodge," in *Earth and Sky*, eds. Williamson and Farrer, 299; Hopman, "Hallucinogens and Rock Art."

11. Froese, Woodward, and Ikegami, "Are Altered States of Consciousness Detrimental," 89–95.

12. Brady and Prufer, "A History of Mesoamerican Cave Interpretation," in *In the Maw of the Earth Monster*, eds. Brady and Prufer, 1–17.

13. Ustinova, *Caves and the Ancient Greek Mind*, 13–52.

14. Simek et al., "Documenting Spatial Order in the Pictograph Panels of Picture Cave," in *Picture Cave*, eds. Diaz-Granados, Duncan, and Reilly, 57–95.

15. Hoffman, *The Midē'wiwin*, 226–227.

16. Brown, "On the Identity of the Birdman within Mississippian Period Art and Iconography," in *Ancient Objects*, eds. Reilly and Gardner, 39–55.

17. Diaz-Granados, "Early Manifestations of Mississippian Iconography in Middle Mississippi Valley Art," in *Visualizing the Sacred*, eds. Lankford, Reilly, and Garber, 64–95.

18. Simek et al., "Documenting Spatial Order in the Pictograph Panels of Picture Cave," in *Picture Cave*, eds. Diaz-Granados, Duncan, and Reilly, 57–95.

19. Knight and Franke, "Identification of a Moth/Butterfly Supernatural in Mississippian Art," in *Ancient Objects*, eds. Reilly and Gardner, 136–151.

20. Lankford, "Some Cosmological Motifs in the Southeastern Ceremonial Complex," in *Ancient Objects*, eds. Reilly and Gardner, 8–38.

21. Lankford, "Visions in Picture Cave," in *Picture Cave*, eds. Diaz-Granados, Duncan, and Reilly, 201–208.

22. Diaz-Granados and Duncan, "Transmogrification, Healing, and Resurrection," in *Picture Cave*, eds. Diaz-Granados, Duncan, and Reilly, 181–187.

23. Lankford, "Was There a Moundville Medicine Society?" in *Rethinking Moundville*, eds. Steponaitis and Scarry, 74–98; Lankford, "Local Eyes: Recognizing Cosmological Motifs," in *New Methods and Theories*, eds. Giles and Lambert, 111–130.

24. Pomedli, *Living with Animals*, 35.

25. Lankford, "Local Eyes: Recognizing Cosmological Motifs," in *New Methods and Theories*, eds. Giles and Lambert, 111–130; Pomedli, *Living with Animals*, 37.

26. Landes, *Ojibwa Religion*, 50–52; Lankford, "Was There a Moundville Medicine Society?" in *Rethinking Moundville*, eds. Steponaitis and Scarry, 74–98.

27. Reilly, "The Great Serpent in the Lower Mississippi Valley," in *Visualizing the Sacred*, eds. Lankford, Reilly, and Garber, 118–134; Reilly, "Foundations and Cosmological Themes in Braden-Style Art," in *Recovering Ancient Spiro*, eds. Singleton and Reilly, 220–233; Lankford, "Weeding Out the Noded," 50–68; Lankford, "Following the Noded Trail," 51–68.

3. A FINGER POINTING AT THE CAHOKIA MOON

1. Pauketat, "The Moon's Tears Fell on Cahokia"; Pauketat, "Lunar Twins"; Romain, "Following the Milky Way Path of Souls," 187–212.

2. Romain, "Crossing to the Land of the Dead"; Romain, "Following the Milky Way Path of Souls," 187–212; Romain, "The Milky Way Path of Souls and Ancient Earthworks in Ohio."

3. Romain, "Monk's Mound as an Axis Mundi for the Cahokian World," 27–52.

4. Brown and Kelly, "The Allure of Cahokia as a Sacred Place in the Eleventh Century." Romain, "Monk's Mound as an Axis Mundi for the Cahokian World."

5. Brown and Kelly, "The Allure of Cahokia as a Sacred Place in the Eleventh Century."

6. Lankford, "Visions in Picture Cave," in *Picture Cave*, eds. Diaz-Granados, Duncan, and Reilly, 201–208.

7. Brown, "Sequencing the Braden Style within Mississippian Period Iconography," in *Ancient Objects*, eds. Reilly and Garber, 213–245.

8. Pauketat, "The Moon's Tears Fell on Cahokia"; Pauketat, "Lunar Twins."

9. Landes, *Ojibwa Religion*, 38.

10. Emerson, "Cahokian Elite Ideology and the Mississippian Cosmos," in *Cahokia*, eds. Emerson and Pauketat, 190–228.

11. Emerson, "Materializing Cahokian Shamans," 135–154.

12. Reilly, "Foundational and Cosmological Themes in Braden-Style Art," in *Recovering Ancient Spiro*, eds. Singleton and Reilly, 220–233.

13. Pauketat, "The Moon's Tears Fell on Cahokia"; Pauketat, "Lunar Twins."

14. Pauketat, "The Moon's Tears Fell on Cahokia"; Pauketat, "Lunar Twins."

15. Pauketat, "The Moon's Tears Fell on Cahokia"; Pauketat, "Lunar Twins."

16. Lisle, *The Stargazer's Guide to the Night Sky*, 83.

17. Pauketat, "The Moon's Tears Fell on Cahokia"; Pauketat, "Lunar Twins."

18. Skousen, "Rethinking Archaeologies of Pilgrimage," 261–283.

19. Pauketat, "The Moon's Tears Fell on Cahokia"; Pauketat, "Lunar Twins."

20. Landes, *Ojibwa Religion*, 118.

21. Landes, *Ojibwa Religion*, 26–27.

22. Landes, *Ojibwa Religion*, 118–122.

23. Pauketat, "The Moon's Tears Fell on Cahokia"; Pauketat, "Lunar Twins."

24. Dye, "Lightning Boy and Thunder Boy," in *Ancestors and Creation*, eds. King and Boles.

25. Brown, "On the Identity of the Birdman within Mississippian Period Art and Iconography," in *Ancient Objects*, eds. Reilly and Gardner, 39–55.

26. Dye, "The Hero Twins in the Lower Mississippi Valley," in *Explanations in Iconography*, ed. Diaz-Granados.

27. Lankford, "The 'Path of Souls': Some Death Imagery in the Southeastern Ceremonial Complex," in *Ancient Objects*, eds. Reilly and Garber, 174–212.

28. Brown, "On the Identity of the Birdman within Mississippian Period Art and Iconography," in *Ancient Objects*, eds. Reilly and Gardner, 39–55.

29. Pauketat, *Ancient Cahokia and the Mississippians*, 63.

30. Pauketat, "Lunar Twins."

31. Rafferty, *Native Intoxicants of North America*, 116.

32. Milanich, "Origins and Prehistoric Distributions of Black Drink and the Ceremonial Shell Drinking Cup," in *Black Drink*, ed. Charles Hudson, 83–119.

33. Hudson, "Introduction," in *Black Drink*, ed. Charles Hudson, 1–9.

34. Rafferty, *Native Intoxicants of North America*, 118–127.

35. Rafferty, *Native Intoxicants of North America*, 122–128.

36. Dieterle, "Grizzlyman as a Preform of Blue Bear."

37. Dieterle, "Grizzlyman as a Preform of Blue Bear."

38. Reilly, "The Art and Iconography of the Ancient American South."

39. Rafferty, *Native Intoxicants of North America*, 123.

40. Hudson, "Introduction," in *Black Drink*, ed. Charles Hudson, 1–9.

41. Rafferty, *Native Intoxicants of North America*, 118–120.

42. Ruxton, *Life in the Far West*, 105.

43. Cutler, *Tracks That Speak*, 174–176; Densmore, *Chippewa Customs*, 144–145.

44. Tushingham and Eerkens, "Hunter-Gatherer Tobacco Smoking in Ancient North America: Current Chemical Evidence and a Framework for Future Studies," in *Perspectives*, eds. Bollwerk and Tushingham, 211–230.

45. Singleton and Reilly, "Introduction," in *Recovering Ancient Spiro*, eds. Singleton and Reilly, 1–15.

4. A LODGE OF SPIRITS AT SPIRO

1. Clements, "Historical Sketch of the Spiro Mound"; Reilly, "The Art and Iconography of the Ancient American South"; Reilly, "Spiro Archaeological Site: Travels on the Path of Souls."

2. Brown, "Spiro Reconsidered: Sacred Economy at the Western Frontier of the Eastern Woodlands," in *Archaeology of the Caddo*, eds. Perttula and Walker 117–138.

3. Regnier, Livingwood, and Hammerstedt, "The History of Spiro," in *Recovering Ancient Spiro*, eds. Singleton and Reilly, 18–33.

4. Lankford, "The Raptor on the Path," in *Visualizing the Sacred*, eds. Lankford, Reilly, and Garber, 240–250.

5. Ruck, Hoffman, and Celdrán, *Mushrooms, Myth and Mithras*, 31.

6. Wasson, Hofmann, and Ruck, *The Road to Eleusis*, 85–136.

7. Reilly, "Spiro Archaeological Site: Travels on the Path of Souls."

8. Brown, Barker, and Sabo, "The Spirit Lodge, Spiro Ritual, and Cosmic Renewal," in *Recovering Ancient Spiro*, eds. Singleton and Reilly, 92–113.

5. LOST MARBLES AT ETOWAH

1. Georgia State Parks and Historic Sites, "Etowah Indian Mounds, State Historic Site, Cartersville."

2. King, "Deciphering Etowah's Mound C: The Construction History and Mortuary Record of a Mississippian Burial Mound."

3. King, *Etowah*, 75.

4. King, *Etowah*, 75.

5. Knight and Franke, "Identification of a Moth/Butterfly Supernatural in Mississippian Art," in *Ancient Objects*, eds. Reilly and Garber, 136–151.

6. Knight and Franke, "Identification of a Moth/Butterfly Supernatural in Mississippian Art," in *Ancient Objects*, eds. Reilly and Garber, 136–151.

7. Larson, "A Mississippian Headdress from Etowah, Georgia," 109–112.

8. Larson, "A Mississippian Headdress from Etowah, Georgia."

9. Larson, "A Mississippian Headdress from Etowah, Georgia," 109–112.

10. Larson, "A Mississippian Headdress from Etowah, Georgia," 109–112.

11. Larson, "A Mississippian Headdress from Etowah, Georgia," 109–112.

12. Larson, "A Mississippian Headdress from Etowah, Georgia," 109–112.

13. Reilly, "The Petaloid Motif: A Celestial Symbolic Locative in the Shell

Art of Spiro," in *Ancient Objects*, eds. Reilly and Garber, 39–55.

14. King, *Etowah*, 76.

15. Steponaitis et al., "The Provenance and Use of Etowah Palettes," 81–106.

16. Sawyer and King, "Nested Bundles within Etowah's Mound C," in *Mississippian Culture Heroes*, ed. Dye, 81–106.

17. Smith and Miller, *Speaking with the Ancestors*, 99–105.

18. Smith and Miller, *Speaking with the Ancestors*, 97.

19. Smith and Miller, *Speaking with the Ancestors*, 9.

20. Tennessee Council for Professional Archaeology, "Tennessee's State Artifact."

21. Stone, *The Jaguar Within*, 85–92.

22. Stone, *The Jaguar Within*, 86.

23. Goodman, "Shamanic Trance Postures," in *Shaman's Path*, ed. Gary Doore, 53–61.

24. Smith and Miller, *Speaking with the Ancestors*, 104.

25. Goodman, "Shamanic Trance Postures," in *Shaman's Path*, ed. Gary Doore, 53–61.

26. Smith and Miller, *Speaking with the Ancestors*, 99.

27. Carmody et al., "Evidence of Tobacco from a Late Archaic Smoking Tube Recovered from the Flint River Site in Southeastern North America," 904–910.

28. Sawyer and King, "Nested Bundles within Etowah's Mound C," in *Mississippian Culture Heroes*, ed. Dye, 81–106.

6. THE NECROPOLIS OF MOUNDVILLE

1. King and Reilly, "Raptor Imagery at Etowah: The Raptor is the Path to Power," in *Visualizing the Sacred*, eds. Lankford, Reilly, and Garber, 313–320.

2. Knight, James Vernon, "An Archaeological Sketch of Moundville," *Moundville Archaeological Museum*, May 5, 2023.

3. Lankford, "Was There a Moundville Medicine Society?" in *Rethinking Moundville*, eds. Steponaitis and Scarry, 74–98.

4. Lankford, "Was There a Moundville Medicine Society?" in *Rethinking Moundville*, eds. Steponaitis and Scarry, 74–98.

5. Pomedli, *Living with Animals*, 110.

6. Wilbert, *Tobacco and Shamanism in South America*, 165–166.

7. Dewdney, *The Sacred Scrolls of the Southern Ojibway*, 104–105.

8. Lankford, "The 'Path of Souls': Some Death Imagery in the Southeastern Ceremonial Complex," in *Ancient Objects*, eds. Reilly and Garber, 174–212.

9. Lankford, "The 'Path of Souls': Some Death Imagery in the Southeastern Ceremonial Complex," in *Ancient Objects*, eds. Reilly and Garber, 174–212; Little, *Path of Souls*, 140–141.

10. Lankford, "The 'Path of Souls': Some Death Imagery in the Southeastern Ceremonial Complex," in *Ancient Objects*, eds. Reilly and Garber, 174–212.

11. Lankford, "The 'Path of Souls': Some Death Imagery in the Southeastern Ceremonial Complex," in *Ancient Objects*, eds. Reilly and Garber, 174–212.

12. Still Smoking, "Tribal Education: A Case Study of Blackfeet Elders."

13. ExplorePAHistory.com, "Iroquois Creation Story."

14. Beke, *Visible Gates*, 9–11.

15. Beke, *Visible Gates*, 13–15.

16. Beke, *Visible Gates in the Pagan Skies*, 9.

17. Hancock, *America Before*, 216–25.

18. Beke, *Visible Gates in the Pagan Skies*, 9.

19. Gardner and Maier, *Gilgamesh*, 198.

20. Black and Green, *Gods, Demons and Symbols of Ancient Mesopotamia*, 49.

21. Collon, *First Impressions*, 35.

22. Beke, *Visible Gates in the Pagan Skies*, 23.

23. Beke, *Visible Gates in the Pagan Skies*, 23–25.

24. Lankford, "The 'Path of Souls': Some Death Imagery in the Southeastern Ceremonial Complex," in *Ancient Objects*, eds. Reilly and Garber, 174–212.

25. Brown, "On the Identity of the Birdman within Mississippian Period Art and Iconography," in *Ancient Objects*, eds. Reilly and Gardner, 39–55.

26. Rafferty, *Native Intoxicants of North America*, 86.

27. Lankford, "The Raptor on the Path," in *Visualizing the Sacred*, eds. Lankford, Reilly, and Garber, 240–250.

28. King and Reilly, "Raptor Imagery at Etowah: The Raptor is the Path to Power," in *Visualizing the Sacred*, eds. Lankford, Reilly, and Garber, 313–320.

29. Lankford, "The Raptor on the Path," in *Visualizing the Sacred*, eds. Lankford, Reilly, and Garber, 240–250.

30. Lankford, "The 'Path of Souls': Some Death Imagery in the Southeastern Ceremonial Complex," in *Ancient Objects*, eds. Reilly and Garber, 174–212.

7. MAGIC PLANTS AND SHAMANISM IN THE MIIS

1. Reilly, "The Great Serpent in the Lower Mississippi Valley," in *Visualizing the Sacred*, eds. Lankford, Reilly, and Garber, 118–134.
2. King et al., "Absorbed Residue Evidence for Prehistoric *Datura* Use in the American Southeast and Western Mexico."
3. Lankford, "The Swirl-Cross and the Center," in *Visualizing the Sacred*, eds. Lankford, Reilly, and Garber, 251–275.
4. Dye, "Earth Mother Cult Ceramic Statuary in the Lower Mississippi Valley."
5. Diaz-Granados and Duncan, "Empowering the SECC: The 'Old Woman' and Oral Tradition," in *The Rock-Art of Eastern North America*, eds. Diaz-Granados and Duncan, 190–218.
6. Sharp, Knight, and Lankford, "Woman in the Patterned Shawl," in *Visualizing the Sacred*, eds. Lankford, Reilly, and Garber, 177–198.
7. Huckell and VanPool, "*Toloatzin* and Shamanic Journeys: Exploring the Ritual Role of Sacred Datura in the Prehistoric Southwest," in *Religion in The Prehispanic Southwest*, eds. VanPool, VanPool, and Phillips Jr., 147–163; Lankford, "Weeding Out the Noded," 50–68; Lankford, "Following the Noded Trail," 51–68.
8. Lankford, "Weeding Out the Noded," 50–68.
9. Lankford, "Weeding Out the Noded," 50–68.
10. Blanton, "Evolution of a Ritual: Pipes and Smoking in Etowah's Realm," in *Perspectives*, eds. Bollwerk and Tushingham, 93–108.
11. Rätsch, *The Encyclopedia of Psychoactive Plants*, 210.
12. Rätsch, *The Encyclopedia of Psychoactive Plants*, 210.
13. Rätsch, *The Encyclopedia of Psychoactive Plants*, 210.
14. Kassabaum and Martin, "Hero Twins of the Americas: Myths of Origins, Duality, and Vengeance."
15. Dye, "Head Pots and Religious Sodalities in the Lower Mississippi Valley," in *Shaman, Priest, Practice, Belief*, eds. Carmody and Barrier, 203–233.
16. Dye, "Head Pots and Religious Sodalities in the Lower Mississippi Valley," in *Shaman, Priest, Practice, Belief*, eds. Carmody and Barrier, 203–233.
17. Knight and Franke, "Identification of a Moth/Butterfly Supernatural in Mississippian Art," in *Ancient Objects*, eds. Reilly and Garber, 136–151.
18. Barksdale, "The Kingdom of Spiro: A Forgotten Civilization."
19. Narby and Pizuri, *Plant Teachers*, 33.

20. Robinson et al., "*Datura* Quids at Pinwheel Cave, California, Provide Unambiguous Confirmation of the Ingestion of Hallucinogens at a Rock Art Site," 31,026–31,037.

21. Glasgow, "Sacred Datura."

22. Blankenship, "Geochemical Analyses of Prehistoric Pigment Materials from Picture Cave," in *Picture Cave*, eds. Diaz-Granados, Duncan, and Reilly, 37–45.

23. De Pastino, "Hallucinogenic Plants May Be Key to Decoding Ancient Southwestern Paintings," *Institut Superieur d'Anthropologie*, 2014.

24. Dieterle, "The Rise of Morning Star," *Hotcak Encyclopedia*.

25. Narby and Pizuri, *Plant Teachers*, 36.

26. Lankford, "Following the Noded Trail," 51–68.

27. Singleton and Reilly, *Recovering Ancient Spiro*.

28. Knight and Franke, "Identification of a Moth/Butterfly Supernatural in Mississippian Art," in *Ancient Objects*, eds. Reilly and Garber, 136–151.

29. Lankford, "The Great Serpent in Eastern North America," in *Ancient Objects*, eds. Reilly and Garber, 107–135.

30. Huckell and VanPool, "*Toloatzin* and Shamanic Journeys: Exploring the Ritual Role of Sacred Datura in the Prehistoric Southwest," in *Religion in The Prehispanic Southwest*, eds. VanPool, VanPool, and Phillips Jr., 147–163.

31. Smith, "Noded Pots, Moths, and the Datura Cult in Middle Tennessee.

32. Huckell and VanPool, "*Toloatzin* and Shamanic Journeys: Exploring the Ritual Role of Sacred Datura in the Prehistoric Southwest," in *Religion in the Prehispanic Southwest*, eds. VanPool, VanPool, and Phillips Jr., 147–163.

33. Barrier, "Psychotropic Plants and Sacred Animals at the Washausen Mound-Town: Religious Ritual and the Early Mississippian Era," in *Shaman, Priest, Practice, Belief*, eds. Carmody and Barrier, 147–165.

34. Hollenbach, "Plant Use at a Mississippian and Contact-Period Site in the South Carolina Coastal Plain"; Parker and Simon, "Magic Plants and Mississippian Ritual," in *Archaeology and Ancient Religion*, eds. Koldehoff and Pauketat, 117–166; Barrier, "Psychotropic Plants and Sacred Animals at the Washausen Mound-Town: Religious Ritual and the Early Mississippian Era," in *Shaman, Priest, Practice, Belief*, eds. Carmody and Barrier, 147–165.

35. Barrier, "Psychotropic Plants and Sacred Animals at the Washausen Mound-Town: Religious Ritual and the Early Mississippian Era," in *Shaman, Priest, Practice, Belief*, eds. Carmody and Barrier, 147–165.

36. Barrier, "Psychotropic Plants and Sacred Animals at the Washausen Mound-

Town: Religious Ritual and the Early Mississippian Era," in *Shaman, Priest, Practice, Belief*, eds. Carmody and Barrier, 147–165.

37. Parker and Simon, "Magic Plants and Mississippian Ritual," in *Archaeology and Ancient Religion*, eds. Koldehoff and Pauketat, 117–166

38. Parker and Simon, "Magic Plants and Mississippian Ritual," in *Archaeology and Ancient Religion*, eds. Koldehoff and Pauketat, 117–166.

39. Barrier, "Psychotropic Plants and Sacred Animals at the Washausen Mound-Town: Religious Ritual and the Early Mississippian Era," in *Shaman, Priest, Practice, Belief*, eds. Carmody and Barrier, 147–165.

40. Pauketat, *Gods of Thunder*, 173–174.

41. Hazzard-Donald, *Mojo Workin'*, 69.

42. Thompson, *Flash of the Spirit*, 131.

43. Parker and Simon, "Magic Plants and Mississippian Ritual," in *Archaeology and Ancient Religion*, eds. Koldehoff and Pauketat, 117–166.

44. Hofmann and Tscherter, "Isolation of Lysergic Acid Alkaloids from the Mexican Drug Ololiuqui (*Rivea corymbosa* (L.) Hall.f.), 414.

45. Schultes, *A Contribution*.

46. Rätsch, *The Encyclopedia of Psychoactive Plants*, 515.

47. Barrier, "Psychotropic Plants and Sacred Animals at the Washausen Mound-Town: Religious Ritual and the Early Mississippian Era," in *Shaman, Priest, Practice, Belief*, eds. Carmody and Barrier, 147–165.

48. Parker and Simon, "Magic Plants and Mississippian Ritual," in *Archaeology and Ancient Religion*, eds. Koldehoff and Pauketat, 117–166.

49. Rätsch, *The Encyclopedia of Psychoactive Plants*, 298.

50. Rätsch, *The Encyclopedia of Psychoactive Plants*, 305.

51. Savage, Harman, and Fadiman, "*Ipomoea purpurea*: A Naturally Occurring Psychedelic," in *Altered States of Consciousness*, ed. Tart.

52. Fang et al., "Tracing the Geographic Origins of Weedy *Ipomoea purpurea* in the Southeastern United States," 666–677.

53. Rätsch, *The Encyclopedia of Psychoactive Plants*, 298–299.

54. Rätsch, *The Encyclopedia of Psychoactive Plants*, 299.

55. Rätsch, *The Encyclopedia of Psychoactive Plants*, 515.

56. Rätsch, *The Encyclopedia of Psychoactive Plants*, 299.

57. Beaulieu et al., "Diversification of Ergot Alkaloids and Heritable Fungal Symbionts in Morning Glories."

58. Parker and Simon, "Magic Plants and Mississippian Ritual," in *Archaeology and Ancient Religion*, eds. Koldehoff and Pauketat, 117–166.

59. Wilkinson, Hardcastle, and McCormick, "Ergot Alkaloid Contents of *Ipomoea lacunosa, I. hederaceae, I. trichocarpa,* and *I. purpurea* seed."

60. Abou-Chaar, "Alkaloids of an *Ipomoea* Seed Known as Kaladana in Pakistan," 618–619.

61. Meira et al., "Review of the Genus *Ipomoea*: Traditional Uses, Chemistry and Biological Activities."

62. Haschek and Voss, "Safety Assessment including Current and Emerging Issues in Toxicologic Pathology," in *Haschek and Rousseaux's Handbook,* eds. Haschek, Rousseaux, and Wallig.

63. Zia-Ul-Haq, Riaz, and De Feo, "*Ipomea hederacea* Jacq.: A Medicinal Herb with Promising Health Benefits," 13, 132–13, 145.

64. Barnouw, *Wisconsin Chippewa Myths and Tales,* 259.

65. Wasson, *Persephone's Quest,* 18.

66. Rätsch, *The Encyclopedia of Psychoactive Plants,* 300.

67. Barnouw, *Wisconsin Chippewa Myths and Tales,* 259.

68. Romain, *Shamans of the Lost World,* 182.

69. Romain, *Shamans of the Lost World,* 182.

70. Densmore, *Chippewa Customs,* 73–75.

71. Rätsch, *The Encyclopedia of Psychoactive Plants,* 635.

72. Heinrich, *Magic Mushrooms in Religion and Alchemy,* 47.

73. Romain, *Mysteries of the Hopewell,* 214.

74. Romain, *Mysteries of the Hopewell,* 214.

75. Romain, *Mysteries of the Hopewell,* 216.

76. Romain, *Mysteries of the Hopewell,* 182.

77. Romain, *Shamans of the Lost World,* 183–184.

78. Romain, *Shamans of the Lost World,* 184.

8. THE *MISSIHUASCA* HYPOTHESIS

1. Mooney, "Myths of the Cherokee."

2. Mooney, "The Cherokee Ball Play," 105–132.

3. *First People of America and Canada—Turtle Island.* "*Asinga ya Tsunsdi* 'Little Men'."

4. Mooney, "Myths of the Cherokee."

5. Rätsch, *The Encyclopedia of Psychoactive Plants,* 772.

6. Rätsch, *The Encyclopedia of Psychoactive Plants,* 363.

7. Rätsch, *The Encyclopedia of Psychoactive Plants,* 710.

8. Barker, "*N,N*-Dimethyltryptamine (DMT), an Endogenous Hallucinogen: Past, Present, and Future Research to Determine Its Role and Function," 536.

9. McKenna, *True Hallucinations*, 45.

10. Hollenbach, "Plant Use at a Mississippian and Contact-Period Site in the South Carolina Coastal Plain," in *Forging Southeastern Identities*, eds. Waselkov and Smith, 157–181; Parker and Simon, "Magic Plants and Mississippian Ritual," in *Archaeology and Ancient Religion*, eds. Koldehoff and Pauketat, 117–166; Barrier, "Psychotropic Plants and Sacred Animals at the Washausen Mound-Town: Religious Ritual and the Early Mississippian Era," in *Shaman, Priest, Practice, Belief*, eds. Carmody and Barrier, 147–165.

11. Berlowitz, Egger, and Cumming, "Monoamine Oxidase Inhibition by Plant-Derived β-Carbolines; Implications for the Psychopharmacology of Tobacco and Ayahuasca."

12. Mota et al., "β-Carboline Alkaloid Harmine Induces DNA Damage and Triggers Apoptosis by a Mitochondrial Pathway: Study In Silico, In Vitro and In Vivo."

13. Williams, DeLorenzo, and Burton, "Monoamine Oxidase (MAO) Inhibitors and Uses Thereof," 2005.

14. Goldin and Salani, "Ayahuasca: What Healthcare Providers Need to Know," 167–173; Fotiou and Gearin, "Purging and the Body in the Therapeutic Use of Ayahuasca"; Domínguez-Clavé et al., "Ayahuasca: Pharmacology, Neuroscience and Therapeutic Potential," 89–101.

15. Mooney, "Myths of the Cherokee."

16. Stauffer and Reilly, "Playing the Apalachee Ballgame in the Fields of the Thunder God: Archaeological and Ideological Evidence for Its Antiquity," in *Prehistoric Games*, ed. Voorhies, 34–47.

17. Reichel-Dolmatoff, *The Shaman and the Jaguar*, 98.

18. Reichel-Dolmatoff, *Beyond the Milky Way*, 13.

19. Warren, "Ghosts of Cultivation Past—Native American Dispersal Legacy Persists in Tree Distribution."

BIBLIOGRAPHY

Abbott, P. J. "American Indian and Alaska Native Aboriginal Use of Alcohol in the United States." *American Indian and Alaska Native Mental Health Research* 7, no. 2 (1996): 1–13.

Abou-Chaar, C. I., and G. A. Digenis. "Alkaloids of an *Ipomoea* seed known as Kaladana in Pakistan." *Nature* 212 (Nov. 1, 1966): 618–619.

Angel, Michael. *Preserving the Sacred: Historical Perspectives on the Ojibwa Midewiwin*. Winnipeg, MB: University of Manitoba Press, 2016.

Bacon, Bennett, Azadeh Khatiri, James Palmer, et al. "An Upper Palaeolithic Proto-Writing System and Phenological Calendar." *Cambridge Archaeological Journal* 33, no. 3 (2023): 371–89.

Barker, Steven A. "*N,N*-Dimethyltryptamine (DMT), an Endogenous Hallucinogen: Past, Present, and Future Research to Determine Its Role and Function." *Frontiers in Neuroscience* 12 (Aug. 6, 2018): 536.

Barksdale, Nick. "The Kingdom of Spiro: A Forgotten Civilization." *Study of Antiquity and the Middle Ages*, May 8, 2021. Podcast.

Barnouw, Victor. *Wisconsin Chippewa Myths and Tales: And Their Relation to Chippewa Life*. Madison, WI: University of Wisconsin Press, 1977.

Beaulieu, Wesley T., Daniel G. Panaccione, Quynh N. Quach, Katy L. Smoot, and Keith Clay. "Diversification of Ergot Alkaloids and Heritable Fungal Symbionts in Morning Glories." *Communications Biology* 4, 1362 (2021).

Beke, George Latura. *Visible Gates in the Pagan Skies*. Scotts Valley, CA: CreateSpace Independent Publishing Platform, 2009.

Benton-Banai, Edward. *The Mishomis Book: The Voice of the Ojibway*. Minneapolis, MN: University of Minnesota Press, 2010.

Berlowitz, Ilana, Klemens Egger, and Paul Cumming. "Monoamine Oxidase Inhibition by Plant-Derived β-Carbolines; Implications for the Psychopharmacology of Tobacco and Ayahuasca." *Frontier Pharmacology* 13 (May 2, 2022). National Center for Biotechnology Information website.

Black, Jeremy, and Anthony Green. *Gods, Demons and Symbols of Ancient Mesopotamia: An Illustrated Dictionary.* Austin, TX: University of Texas Press, 2003.

Bollwerk, Elizabeth A., and Shannon Tushingham, eds. *Perspectives on the Archaeology of Pipes, Tobacco and Other Smoke Plants in the Ancient Americas.* New York: Springer, 2016.

Borek, Theodore, Curtis Mowry, and Glenna Dean. "Analysis of Modern and Ancient Artifacts for the Presence of Corn Beer; Dynamic Headspace Testing of Pottery Sherds from Mexico and New Mexico." *MRS Proceedings* 1047 (2007): 1047-Y01-05.

Brady, James E., and Keith M. Prufer, eds. *In the Maw of the Earth Monster: Mesoamerican Ritual Cave Use.* Austin, TX: University of Texas Press, 2005.

Brown, James A., and John E. Kelly. "The Allure of Cahokia as a Sacred Place in the Eleventh Century." ResearchGate, February 2018.

Carmody, Stephen B., and Casey R. Barrier, eds. *Shaman, Priest, Practice, Belief: Materials of Ritual and Religion in Eastern North America.* Tuscaloosa, AL: University of Alabama Press, 2020.

Carmody, S., J. Davis, S. Tadi, et al. "Evidence of Tobacco from a Late Archaic Smoking Tube Recovered from the Flint River Site in Southeastern North America." *Journal of Archaeological Science: Reports* 21 (Oct. 2018): 904–910.

Carr, Christopher. *Being Scioto Hopewell: Ritual Drama and Personhood in Cross-Cultural Perspective.* New York: Springer, 2021.

Cherrington. "Aborigines of North America." In *Standard Encyclopedia of the Alcohol Problem*, vol. I, edited by E. H. Cherrington, 3–42. Westerville, OH: 1925.

Clements, Forest E. "Historical Sketch of the Spiro Mound." 1945. Museum of the American Indian/Heye Foundation Records, 1890–1989, Box 413, Folder 16. National Museum of the American Indian Archive Center, Smithsonian Institution.

Collon, Dominique. *First Impressions: Cylinder Seals in the Ancient Near East.* London: British Museum Press, 2003.

Cutler, Charles L. *Tracks That Speak: The Legacy of Native American Words in North American Culture*. Boston: Houghton Mifflin Harcourt, 2002.

Densmore, Frances. *Chippewa Customs*. Saint Paul, MN: Minnesota Historical Society Press, 1979.

De Pastino, Blake. "Hallucinogenic Plants May Be Key to Decoding Ancient Southwestern Paintings." Institut Superieur d'Anthropologie website. First published on Western Digs, October 20, 2014 (website discontinued).

Dewdney, Selwyn H. *The Sacred Scrolls of the Southern Ojibway*. Toronto, ON: University of Toronto Press, 1975.

Diaz-Granados, Carol, James R. Duncan, and F. Kent Reilly III, eds. *Picture Cave: Unraveling the Mysteries of the Mississippian Cosmos*. Austin, TX: University of Texas Press, 2015.

Diaz-Granados, Carol, and James R. Duncan, eds. *The Rock-Art of Eastern North America: Capturing Images and Insight*. Tuscaloosa, AL: University of Alabama Press, 2004.

Dieterle, Richard L. "The Rise of Morning Star: The Role of Theological Astronomy in the Cultural Revolution of the XITH Century." Hotcak Encyclopedia. Accessed July 30, 2024.

Dieterle, Richard L. "Grizzlyman as a Preform of Blue Bear." Hotcak Encyclopedia. Accessed July 30, 2024.

Domínguez-Clavé, E., J. Soler, M. Elices, et al. "Ayahuasca: Pharmacology, Neuroscience and Therapeutic Potential." *Brain Research Bulletin* 126, pt. 1 (September 2016): 89–101.

Doore, Gary, ed. *Shaman's Path: Healing, Personal Growth, and Empowerment*. Boulder, CO: Shambhala, 1988.

Dye, David H. "Earth Mother Cult Ceramic Statuary in the Lower Mississippi Valley." Presented in the symposium "Statues and Statuettes in the Mississippian Period: Bridges to Other Worlds" at the 72nd Annual Meeting of the Southeastern Archaeological Conference, Nashville, Tennessee, November 19, 2015.

———. "The Hero Twins in the Lower Mississippi Valley." In *Explanations in Iconography: Ancient American Indian Art, Symbol, and Meaning*, edited by Carol Diaz-Granados. Havertown, PA: Oxbow Books. 2023.

———. "Lightning Boy and Thunder Boy." In *Ancestors and Creation: The Symbolism and Founding Ideologies of Mississippian Belief Systems*, edited by

Adam King and Steven Boles. Gainesville, FL: University Press of Florida, forthcoming.

———, ed. *Mississippian Culture Heroes, Ritual Regalia, and Sacred Bundles.* Lanham, MD: Lexington Books, 2021.

Emerson, Thomas E. "Materializing Cahokian Shamans." *Southeastern Archaeology* 22, no. 2 (2003): 135–154.

Emerson, Thomas E., and Timothy R. Pauketat, eds. *Cahokia: Domination and Ideology in the Mississippian World.* Lincoln, NE: University of Nebraska Press, 1997.

Fang, Zhou, Ana M. Gonzales, Mary L. Durbin, et al. "Tracing the Geographic Origins of Weedy *Ipomoea purpurea* in the Southeastern United States." *Journal of Heredity* 104, no. 5 (September–October 2013): 666–677.

Fotiou, Evengia, and Alex K. Gearin. "Purging and the Body in the Therapeutic Use of Ayahuasca." *Social Science and Medicine* 239 (October 2019). National Center for Biotechnology Information website.

Frank, John W, Roland S. Moore, and Genevieve M. Ames, "Historical and Cultural Roots of Drinking Problems among American Indians." *American Journal of Public Health* 90, no. 3, 344–351.

Freidel, David, Linda Schele, and Joy Parker. *Maya Cosmos: Three Thousand Years on the Shaman's Path.* New York: HarperCollins, 2001.

Froese T., A. Woodward, and T. Ikegami. "Are Altered States of Consciousness Detrimental, Neutral or Helpful for the Origins of Symbolic Cognition? A Response to Hodgson and Lewis-Williams." *Adaptive Behavior* 22, no. 1 (2014): 89–95.

Gardner, John, ed., and John Maier, trans. *Gilgamesh.* New York: Knopf Publishing Company, 1984.

Georgia State Parks and Historic Sites, "Etowah Indian Mounds, State Historic Site, Cartersville." Accessed July 30, 2024.

Giles, Bretton T., and Shawn P. Lambert, eds. *New Methods and Theories for Analyzing Mississippian Imagery.* Gainesville, FL: University of Florida Press, 2021.

Glasgow, Karla. "Sacred Datura." *Preservation Archaeology Blog,* June 21, 2017.

Goldin and Salani. "Ayahuasca: What Healthcare Providers Need to Know." *Journal of Addictions Nursing* 32, no. 2 (April 2021), 167–173.

Grim, John A. *The Shaman: Patterns of Religious Healing among the Ojibway Indians.* Norman, OK: University of Oklahoma Press, 1987.

Hancock, Graham. *America Before: The Key to Earth's Lost Civilization*. London: Hodder & Stoughton, 2019.

Haschek, Wanda M., and Kenneth A. Voss. "Safety Assessment including Current and Emerging Issues in Toxicologic Pathology." In *Haschek and Rousseaux's Handbook of Toxicologic Pathology*, edited by Wanda Haschek, Colin G. Rousseaux, and Matthew A. Wallig. Amsterdam: Elsevier Science, 2013.

Hazzard-Donald, Katrina. *Mojo Workin': The Old African American Hoodoo System*. Champaign, IL: University of Illinois Press, 2013.

Heinrich, Clark. *Magic Mushrooms in Religion and Alchemy*. Rochester, VT: Park Street Press, 2002.

Hoffman, Walter James. *The Midē'wiwin: Grand Medicine Society of the Ojibway*. Honolulu: University Press of the Pacific, 2005.

Hofmann, A., and Tscherter, H. "Isolation of Lysergic Acid Alkaloids from the Mexican Drug Ololiuqui (*Rivea corymbosa* (L.) Hall.f.). *Experientia*, nos. 15 and 16 (September 1960): 414.

Hollenbach, Kandace D. "Plant Use at a Mississippian and Contact-Period Site in the South Carolina Coastal Plain." In *Forging Southeastern Identities: Social Archaeology, Ethnohistory, and Folklore of the Mississippian to Early Historic South*, eds. Gregory A. Waselkov and Marvin T. Smith. Tuscaloosa, AL: University of Alabama Press, 2017.

Hopman, Eva. "Hallucinogens and Rock Art: Altered States of Consciousness in the Palaeolithic Period." Paper, University of Groningen Institute of Archaeology, 2008. Available at Academia.edu website.

Howey, Meghan C.L., and John M. O'Shea. "Bear's Journey and the Study of Ritual in Archaeology." *American Antiquity* 71. no. 2 (April 2006): 261–282.

Hudson, Charles M., ed. *Black Drink: A Native American Tea*. Athens, GA: University of Georgia Press, 2004.

Hultkrantz, Åke. *The North American Indian Orpheus Tradition: Native Afterlife Myths and Their Origins*. Santa Fe: Afterworlds Press, 2022.

Jay, Mike. *Mescaline: A Global History of the First Psychedelic*. New Haven: Yale University Press, 2019.

Johnston, Basil. *Ojibway Ceremonies*. Lincoln, NE: University of Nebraska Press, 1990.

Kassabaum, Megan, and Simon Martin. "Hero Twins of the Americas: Myths of Origins, Duality, and Vengeance." Lecture, Penn Museum Lecture Series: Exploring Great Myths and Legends, February 3, 2016.

Keck, Gayle. "The Altered States of America." *American Archaeology* 25, no.2 (Summer 2022): 33–39.

Kinietz, W. Vernon. *Chippewa Village: The Story of Katikitegon*. Bloomfield Hills, MI: Cranbrook Institute of Science, 1947.

Koldehoff, Brad H., and Timothy R. Pauketat, eds. *Archaeology and Ancient Religion in the American Midcontinent*. Tuscaloosa, AL: University of Alabama Press, 2018.

King. "Deciphering Etowah's Mound C: The Construction History and Mortuary Record of a Mississippian Burial Mound." *Southeastern Archaeology* 23, no. 2 (Winter 2004): 153–165.

King, Adam, Terry G. Powis, Kong F. Cheong, et al. "Absorbed Residue Evidence for Prehistoric *Datura* Use in the American Southeast and Western Mexico." *Advances in Archaeological Practice* 6, no. 4 (2018): 312–27.

Knight, James Vernon. "An Archaeological Sketch of Moundville." Published at *Moundville Archaeological Museum*. May 5, 2023.

Lanaud, Claire, Hélène Vignes, José Utge, et al. "A Revisited History of Cacao Domestication in Pre-Columbian Times Revealed by Archaeogenomic Approaches." *Scientific Reports* 14 (2024). *Nature* website.

Landes, Ruth. *Ojibwa Religion and the Midewiwin*. Madison, WI: University of Wisconsin Press, 1968.

Lane, Tom. *Sacred Mushroom Rituals: The Search for the Blood of Quetzalcoatl*. Gainesville, FL: Solarwolf Publications, 2018.

Lankford, George E. *Native American Legends of the Southeast: Tales from the Natchez, Caddo, Biloxi, Chickasaw, and Other Nations*. Tuscaloosa, AL: University of Alabama Press, 2011.

———. *Reachable Stars: Patterns in the Ethnoastronomy of Eastern North America*. Tuscaloosa, AL: University of Alabama Press, 2007.

———. "Following the Noded Trail." *The Arkansas Archaeologist* 53 (2014): 51–68.

———. "Weeding Out the Noded." *The Arkansas Archaeologist* 50 (2010): 50–68.

Lankford, George E., F. Kent Reilly III, and James F. Garber, eds. *Visualizing the Sacred: Cosmic Visions, Regionalism, and the Art of the Mississippian World*. Austin, TX: University of Texas Press, 2011.

Larson, Lewis H. "A Mississippian Headdress from Etowah, Georgia." *American Antiquity* 25, no. 1 (July 1959): 109–112.

Lisle, Jason. *The Stargazer's Guide to the Night Sky*. Green Forest, AR: Master Books, 2012.

Little, Gregory. *Path of Souls: The Native American Death Journey*. Memphis, TN: ATA-Archetype Books, 2014.

Mancall, Peter C. *Deadly Medicine: Indians and Alcohol in Early America*. Ithaca, NY: Cornell University Press, 1997.

McKenna, Terence. *True Hallucinations: Being an Account of the Author's Extraordinary Adventures in the Devil's Paradise*. San Francisco: HarperOne, 1994.

Meira, Marilena, Eliezer Pereira da Silva, Jorge Mauricio David, et al. "Review of the Genus *Ipomoea*: Traditional Uses, Chemistry and Biological Activities." SciELO Brazil (website), 2012.

Mooney, James. *Myths of the Cherokee (Unabridged)*. N.p.: Everest Media LLC, 2024. Ebook.

———. "The Cherokee Ball Play." *American Anthropologist* 3, no. 2 (April 1890): 105–132.

Mota, Nadia S. R. S, Maicon R. Kviecinski, Karina B. Felipe, et al. "β-Carboline Alkaloid Harmine Induces DNA Damage and Triggers Apoptosis by a Mitochondrial Pathway: Study In Silico, In Vitro and In Vivo." ResearchGate, May 2020.

Myerhoff, Barbera G. *Peyote Hunt: The Sacred Journey of the Huichol Indians*. Ithaca, NY: Cornell University Press, 1974.

Narby, Jeremy, and Raphael Chanchari Pizuri. *Plant Teachers: Ayahuasca, Tobacco, and the Pursuit of Knowledge*. Novato, CA: New World Library, 2021.

National Association of Exporters and Industrialists of Cacao of Ecuador website. "History of Cacao." Accessed July 30, 2024.

National Park Service website. "Prehistoric Cave Discoveries." Accessed July 30, 2024.

National Park Service website. "Solution Caves." Accessed July 30, 2024.

Naydler, Jeremy. *Temple of the Cosmos: The Ancient Egyptian Experience of the Sacred*. Rochester, VT: Inner Traditions International, 1996.

Pauketat, Timothy R. *Ancient Cahokia and the Mississippians*. Cambridge, UK: Cambridge University Press, 2004.

———. "Lunar Twins: Cahokia's Emerald Acropolis & Chaco's Chimney Rock in the 11th Century." *Discover Archaeology Webinar Series*. Crow Canyon Archaeological Center, May 5, 2022. YouTube video.

———. "The Moon's Tears Fell on Cahokia." *Virtual Lecture Series 2021*. The Archaeological Conservancy, November 11, 2021. YouTube video.

———. *Gods of Thunder: How Climate Change, Travel, and Spirituality Reshaped Precolonial America*. New York: Oxford University Press, 2023.

Pauketat, Timothy R., and Susan M. Alt, eds. *Medieval Mississippians: The Cahokian World*. Santa Fe: School for Advanced Research Press, 2015.

Perttula, Timothy K., and Chester P. Walker, eds. *The Archaeology of the Caddo*. Lincoln, NE: University of Nebraska Press, 2012.

Peschel, Keewaydinoquay Pakawakuk. "The Legend of Miskwedo." *Journal of Psychedelic Drugs* 11 (1–2): 1979, 29–31.

Pomedli, Michael. *Living with Animals: Ojibwe Spirit Powers*. Toronto: University of Toronto Press, 2014.

Rafferty, Sean. *Native Intoxicants of North America*. Knoxville, TN: University of Tennessee Press, 2021.

Rätsch, Christian. *The Encyclopedia of Psychoactive Plants: Ethnopharmacology and Its Applications*. Rochester, VT: Park Street Press, 2005.

Reichel-Dolmatoff, Gerardo. *Beyond the Milky Way: Hallucinatory Imagery of the Tukano Indians*. Los Angeles: UCLA Latin American Center, 1978.

———. *The Shaman and the Jaguar: A Study of Narcotic Drugs Among the Indians of Colombia*. Philadelphia: Temple University Press, 1975.

Reilly, F. Kent. "Spiro Archaeological Site: Travels on the Path of Souls." Lecture, SAR School for Advanced Research, April 11, 2019.

———. "The Art and Iconography of the Ancient American South." Lecture, Center for the Study of the American South. 2018. Delivered to the Center for the Study of the American South on October 2, 2017.

Reilly, F. Kent, III, and James F. Garber, eds. *Ancient Objects and Sacred Realms: Interpretations of Mississippian Iconography*. Austin, TX: University of Texas Press, 2007.

Robinson, David R., Kelly Brown, Moira McMenemy, et al. "*Datura* Quids at Pinwheel Cave, California, Provide Unambiguous Confirmation of the Ingestion of Hallucinogens at a Rock Art Site." *Proceedings of the National Academy of Sciences* 117, no. 49 (2020): 31,026–31,037.

Romain, William F. *Mysteries of the Hopewell: Astronomers, Geometers, and Magicians of the Eastern Woodlands*. Akron, OH: University of Akron Press, 2000.

———. *Shamans of the Lost World: A Cognitive Approach to the Prehistoric Religion of the Ohio Hopewell*. Lanham, MD: AltaMira Press, 2011.

———. "Crossing to the Land of the Dead." Paper presented at the Theoretical Archaeology Group conference, 2021. Academia.edu website.

———. "Following the Milky Way Path of Souls." *Journal of Skyscape Archaeology* 7, no. 2 (2021): 187–212.

———. "Monk's Mound as an Axis Mundi for the Cahokian World." *Illinois Archaeology* 29 (2017): 27–52.

———. "The Milky Way Path of Souls and Ancient Earthworks in Ohio." Presented at the Society for American Archaeology conference, 2016. Academia.edu website.

Rothenberg, Jerome, and Diane Rothenberg, eds. *Symposium of the Whole: A Range of Discourse Toward an Ethnopoetics*. Berkeley, CA: University of California Press, 1983.

Ruck, Carl A. P., Mark Hoffman, and Jose Alfredo Gonzáles Celdrán. *Mushrooms, Myth and Mithras: The Drug Cult That Civilized Europe*. San Francisco: City Lights Publishers, 2011.

Ruxton, George Frederick. *Life in the Far West*. Norman, OK: University of Oklahoma Press, 1951.

Schultes, Richard Evan. *A Contribution to Our Knowledge of Rivea Corymbosa: The Narcotic Ololiuqui of the Aztecs*. Cambridge, MA: Botanical Museum of Harvard University, 1941.

Schultes, Richard Evans, Albert Hofmann, and Christian Rätsch. *Plants of the Gods: Their Sacred, Healing, and Hallucinogenic Powers*. Rochester, VT: Healing Arts Press, 2001.

Schuon, Frithjof. *The Feathered Sun: Plains Indians in Art and Philosophy*. Bloomington, IN: World Wisdom Books, 1990.

Singleton, Eric D., and F. Kent Reilly III, eds. *Recovering Ancient Spiro: Native American Art, Ritual, and Cosmic Renewal*. Oklahoma City, OK: National Cowboy and Western Heritage Museum, 2020.

Skousen, Jacob. "Rethinking Archaeologies of Pilgrimage." *Journal of Social Archaeology* 18, no. 3 (October 2, 2018): 261–283.

Smith, Kevin E. "Noded Pots, Moths, and the Datura Cult in Middle Tennessee." *Middle Cumberland Archaeological Society* Newsletter, 2018. Available at Academia.edu (website).

Smith, Kevin E., and James V. Miller. *Speaking with the Ancestors: Mississippian*

Statuary of the Tennessee-Cumberland Region. Tuscaloosa, AL: University of Alabama Press, 2009.

Steponaitis, Vincas P., Samuel E. Swanson, George Wheeler, et al. "The Provenance and Use of Etowah Palettes." *American Antiquity* 76, no. 1 (January 2011): 81–106.

Steponaitis, Vincas P., and C. Margaret Scarry, eds. *Rethinking Moundville and Its Hinterland.* Gainesville, FL: University of Florida Press, 2016.

Stewart, Tamara. "Ceramic Analysis Indicates Fermented Beverage Was Consumed in New Mexico." *American Archaeology* 12, no. 1 (Spring 2008): 10.

Still Smoking. "Tribal Education: A Case Study of Blackfeet Elders." Ph.D. diss., Montana State University, 1997.

Strieber, Whitley. "Greg Little in a Major Breakthrough." *Dreamland*, September 26, 2014. Podcast.

Stone, Rebecca R. *The Jaguar Within: Shamanic Trance in Ancient Central and South American Art.* Austin, TX: University of Texas Press, 2011.

Sullivan, Lynne P., and Robert C. Mainfort Jr., eds. *Mississippian Mortuary Practices: Beyond Hierarchy and the Representationist Perspective.* Gainesville, FL: University of Florida Press, 2012.

Tart, Charles, ed. *Altered States of Consciousness, A Book of Readings.* Hoboken, NJ: John Wiley and Sons, 1969.

Tennessee Council for Professional Archaeology website. "Tennessee's State Artifact." Accessed July 30, 2024.

Thompson, Robert Farris. *Flash of the Spirit: African and Afro-American Art and Philosophy.* New York: Knopf Doubleday, 2010.

Townsend, Richard F., and Robert V. Sharp, eds. *Hero, Hawk, and Open Hand: American Indian Art of the Ancient Midwest and South.* New Haven: Yale University Press, 2004.

Trenk, Marin. "Religious Uses of Alcohol Among the Woodland Indians of North America." *Anthropos* 96, no. 1 (2001): 73–86.

Ustinova, Yulia. *Caves and the Ancient Greek Mind: Descending Underground in the Search for Ultimate Truth.* Oxford: Oxford University Press, 2009.

VanPool, Christine S. "The Shaman-Priests of the Casas Grandes Region, Chihuahua, Mexico." *American Antiquity* 68, no. 4 (October 2003): 696–717.

VanPool, Christine S., Todd L. VanPool, and David A. Phillips Jr., eds. *Religion in the Prehispanic Southwest.* Lanham, MD: AltaMira Press, 2006.

VanPool, Christine S., and Todd L. VanPool. *Signs of the Casas Grandes Shamans*. Salt Lake City: University of Utah Press, 2007.

Voorhies, Barbara. *Prehistoric Games of North American Indians: Subarctic to Mesoamerica*. Salt Lake City: University of Utah Press, 2017.

Warren, Robert J., II. "Ghosts of Cultivation Past—Native American Dispersal Legacy Persists in Tree Distribution." *PLOS ONE* 11, no. 3 (March 16, 2016): e0150707.

Waselkov, Gregory A., and Marvin T. Smith, eds. *Forging Southeastern Identities: Social Archaeology, Ethnohistory, and Folklore of the Mississippian to Early Historic South*. Tuscaloosa, AL: University of Alabama Press, 2017.

Wasson, R. Gordon, Stella Kramrisch, Johnathan Ott, and Carl A. P. Ruck. *Persephone's Quest: Entheogens and the Origins of Religion*. New Haven: Yale University Press, 1986.

Wasson, R. Gordon, Albert Hofmann, and Carl A. P. Ruck. *The Road to Eleusis: Unveiling the Secret of the Mysteries*. Berkeley, CA: North Atlantic Books, 2008.

Wilbert, Johannes. *Tobacco and Shamanism in South America*. New Haven: Yale University Press, 1987.

Wilkinson, R. E., W. S. Hardcastle, and C. S. McCormick. "Ergot Alkaloid Contents of *Ipomoea lacunosa*, *I. hederaceae*, *I. trichocarpa*, and *I. purpurea* Seed." *Canadian Journal of Plant Science* 66, no. 2 (April 1986): 339–343.

Williams, Jonnie, Robert DeLorenzo, and Harold Burton. "Monoamine Oxidase (MAO) Inhibitors and Uses Thereof." U.S. Patent US6929811B2, filed 2005.

Williamson, Ray A. and Claire R. Farrer, eds. *Earth and Sky: Visions of the Cosmos in Native American Folklore*. Albuquerque, NM: University of New Mexico Press, 1992.

Zia-Ul-Haq, Muhammad, Muhammad Riaz, and Vincenzo De Feo. "*Ipomea hederacea* Jacq.: A Medicinal Herb with Promising Health Benefits." *Molecules* 17, no. 11 (November 5 2012): 13,132–13, 145.

INDEX

Page references in *italics* refer to illustrations.

BOOKS OF RELATED INTEREST

Theurgy: Theory and Practice
The Mysteries of the Ascent to the Divine
by P. D. Newman

Advanced Civilizations of Prehistoric America
The Lost Kingdoms of the Adena, Hopewell, Mississippians, and Anasazi
by Frank Joseph

Sacred Plant Medicine
The Wisdom in Native American Herbalism
by Stephen Harrod Buhner
Foreword by Brooke Medicine Eagle

Rediscovering Turtle Island
A First Peoples' Account of the Sacred Geography of America
by Taylor Keen

The Lost Continent of Pan
The Oceanic Civilization at the Origin of World Culture
by Susan B. Martinez, Ph.D.

Seeding Consciousness
Plant Medicine, Ancestral Wisdom, and Psychedelic Initiation
by Tricia Eastman
Foreword by Alex Grey and Allyson Grey

The Poison Path Grimoire
Dark Herbalism, Poison Magic, and Baneful Allies
by Coby Michael

How Psychedelics Can Help Save the World
Visionary and Indigenous Voices Speak Out
Edited by Stephen Gray
Foreword by Julie Holland, M.D.

INNER TRADITIONS • BEAR & COMPANY
P.O. Box 388
Rochester, VT 05767
1-800-246-8648
www.InnerTraditions.com

Or contact your local bookseller